T5-AOA-150

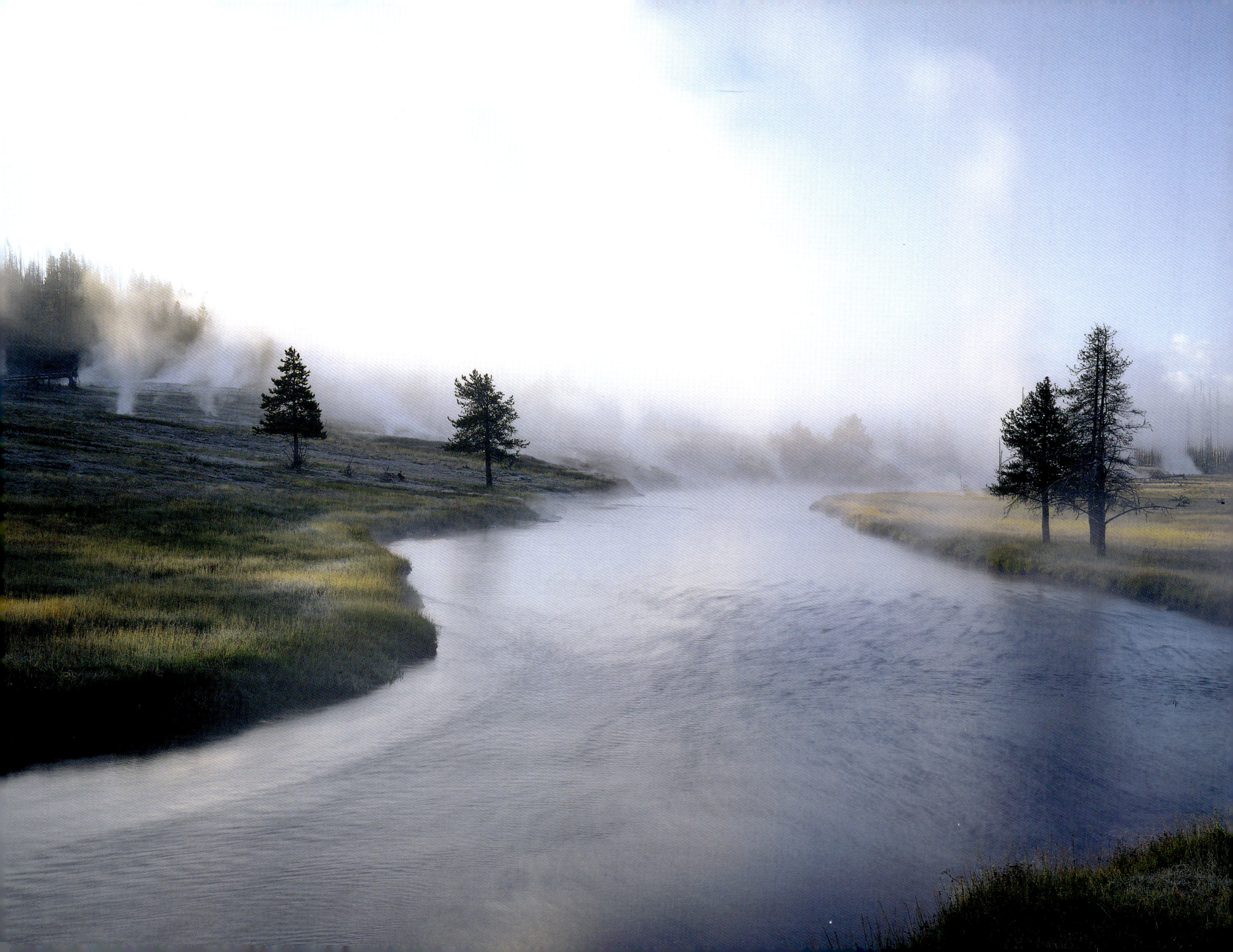

Along Wyoming's Continental Divide Trail

Text and Photography
by Scott T. Smith

WESTCLIFFE PUBLISHERS

www.westcliffepublishers.com

Contents

Acknowledgments 6
Foreword 8
Introduction 10

Sierra Madre

Huston Park Wilderness 13
Bridger Peak 16

Great Divide Basin

Atlantic Rim 27
Ferris Dunes 30

Wind River Range

Cross Lake 45
Pole Creek 51

Greater Yellowstone

Teton Wilderness 65
Old Faithful 76

Appendices 86
History of the Continental Divide
 National Scenic Trail 87

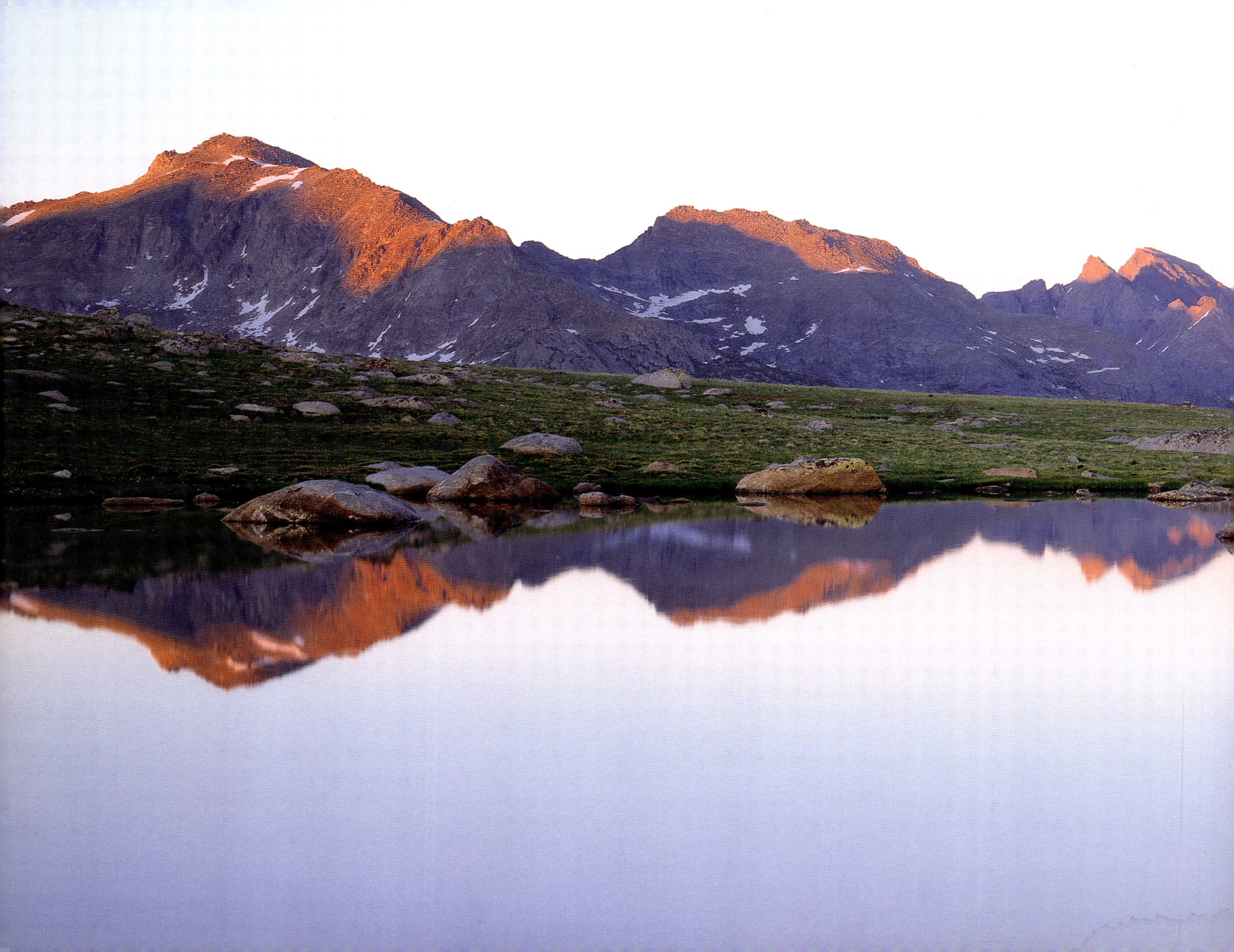

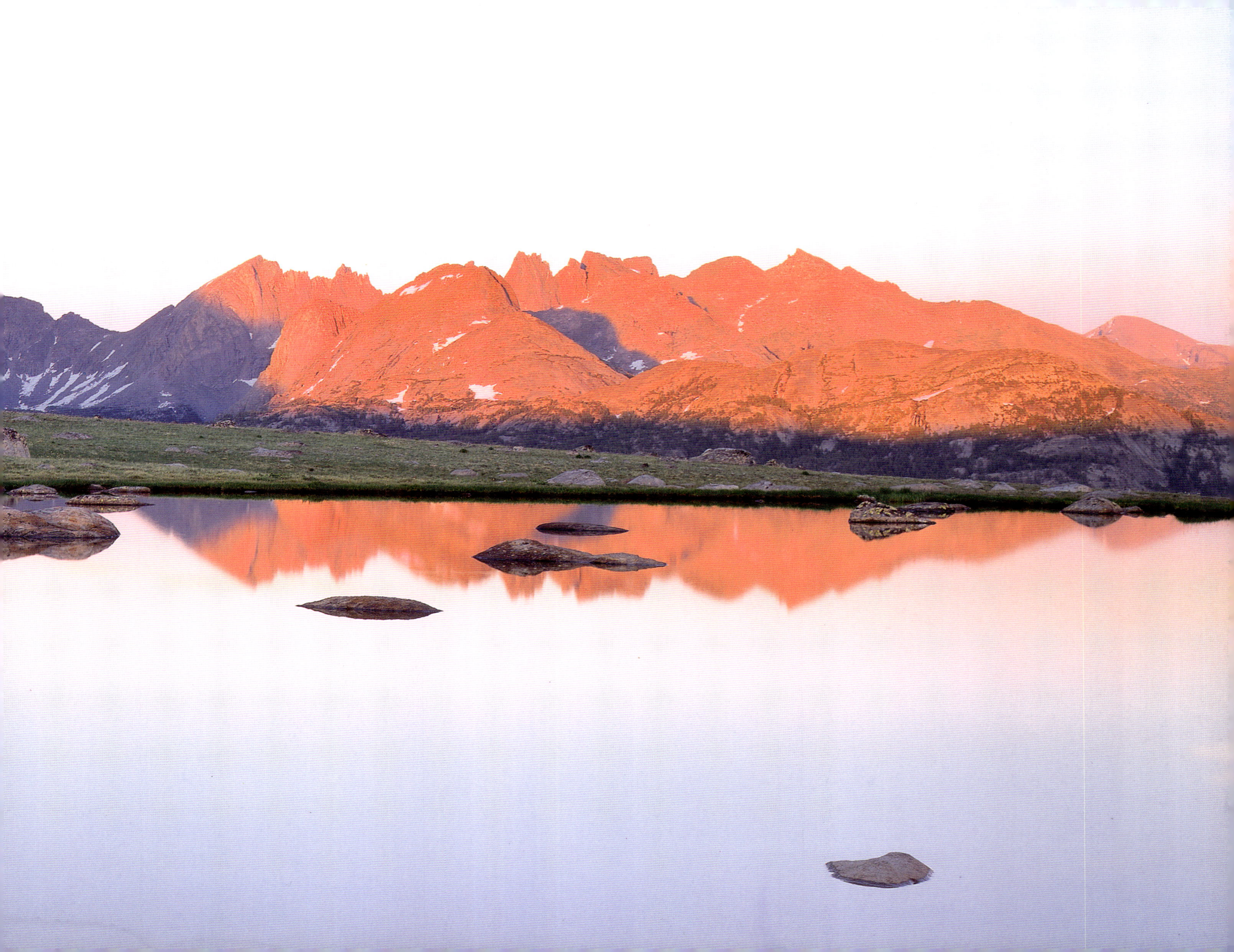

*This book is dedicated to my nephews and nieces: Lucas, Riley, Sean, Jessica, Kelli, and Casey.
May there always be wild trails for you to walk.*

· Acknowledgments ·

Leaving home and office for extended periods of time to photograph and explore a 500-mile-long stretch of trail requires a great deal of help to keep things going (relatively) smoothly. Putting a book together is not done without assistance. I owe debts of gratitude to many people who helped in various ways to produce this volume.

First and foremost, I wish to thank my wife, Mary Bedingfieldsmith. Without her support I would not be working as a photographer at all. She plans trips, wrangles llamas, tends camp, assists with photography, holds down the fort, brings in a steady paycheck, gently criticizes my writing, and is my best friend.

Thanks to my other trail companions: My sister and her husband, Shanna and Doug Moler, took a break from sailing to join us for a most enjoyable summer. Scott Datwyler had his first experience with llamas and found the critters good. Steve Kyriopoulos, who introduced me to llamas years ago, put together a trip where I got to see what a 10-llama pack string looks like. Without "Da Boys"—my llamas Poncho, Cronus, Rocket, and Iago—long wilderness trips with large-format camera gear would be impossible. Thanks, Boys.

Lora Davis helped enormously. The information she gathered as she traveled the entire Wyoming portion of the trail to write *Wyoming's Continental Divide Trail: The Official Guide* was invaluable in planning my trips and writing these stories. She accompanied me on a jeep-trail exploration of potential trail routes in the Great Divide Basin and later put together a memorable snowmobile outing. That motorized winter trip was a success thanks to Steve Faerber at The Resort at Louis Lake, who put us up in his cabin and rode with us; Jay Nolde and Rick Bezanson of Atlantic City Expeditions, who provided snowmobiles; and Jim Smail of the Wyoming State Snowmobile Program, who guided us and was a bottomless well of information.

The land managers, staffers, and rangers at Yellowstone National Park, the Forest Service, and Bureau of Land Management were invariably helpful. Officials at Yellowstone made an exception and let us camp with llamas at a non-stock site so I could have a better opportunity for photos. Rebecca Fitzwilliams and Judy Robinson of the Teton National Forest's Black Rock Ranger District went far beyond the call of duty and shuttled our truck and trailer from Yellowstone to Turpin Meadows.

Thanks to Coleman® for the lantern and stove, and SunDog for the superb photo backpack. Both are Continental Divide Trail Alliance corporate sponsors.

I owe a big debt of gratitude to our neighbors, Don and Patty Johnson, who feed our cats, geese, and any llamas left behind. They water the garden and look after things when we are gone.

John Botkin and the folks at Photo Craft Labs in Boulder, Colorado, do a great job. They make sure my film gets processed right.

And of course, many thanks to John Fielder, Linda Doyle, Jenna Samelson, Craig Keyzer, Pauline Brown, and all the staff at Westcliffe Publishers for producing outstanding books and for allowing me to create this one.

—*Scott T. Smith*

*Part of the proceeds from the sale of this book benefit
the Continental Divide Trail Alliance.*

International Standard Book Number: 1-56579-345-5
Text and Photography Copyright: Scott T. Smith, 2000. All rights reserved.

Editor: Jenna Samelson
Designer: Pauline Brown
Production Manager: Craig Keyzer

Published By:
Westcliffe Publishers, Inc.
P.O. Box 1261
Englewood, CO 80150
www.westcliffepublishers.com

Printed in Hong Kong through World Print, Ltd.

No portion of this book, either text or photography, may be reproduced in any form, including electronically, without the express written permission of the publisher.

Library of Congress Cataloging-in-Publication Data:
Smith, Scott T.
   Along Wyoming's Continental Divide Trail / photography and text by Scott T. Smith.
   p. cm.
   ISBN 1-56579-345-5
   1. Backpacking--Wyoming--Guidebooks. 2. Backpacking--Wyoming--Pictorial works.
3. Backpacking--Continental Divide National Scenic Trail--Guidebooks. 4. Backpacking--Continental Divide National Scenic Trail--Pictorial works. I. Title.

GV199.42.W8 S65 2000
917.87'20434--dc21   00-025079

For more information about other fine books and calendars from Westcliffe Publishers, please contact your local bookstore, call us at 1-800-523-3692, write for our free color catalog, or visit us on the Web at **www.westcliffepublishers.com**.

*First Frontispiece: Island Lake at sunrise. Fremont Peak stands prominently in the distance.
Bridger Wilderness, Wind River Range, Bridger-Teton National Forest.*

Second Frontispiece: Steam from geothermal features rises above the Firehole River at sunrise. Yellowstone National Park.

*Third Frontispiece: The Wind River peaks reflect in a tarn along the Continental Divide at sunset.
Bridger Wilderness, Bridger-Teton National Forest.*

*Opposite: The setting sun casts a glow on the rabbitbrush and rippled sand of the Killpecker Dunes.
Killpecker Dunes Wilderness Study Area.*

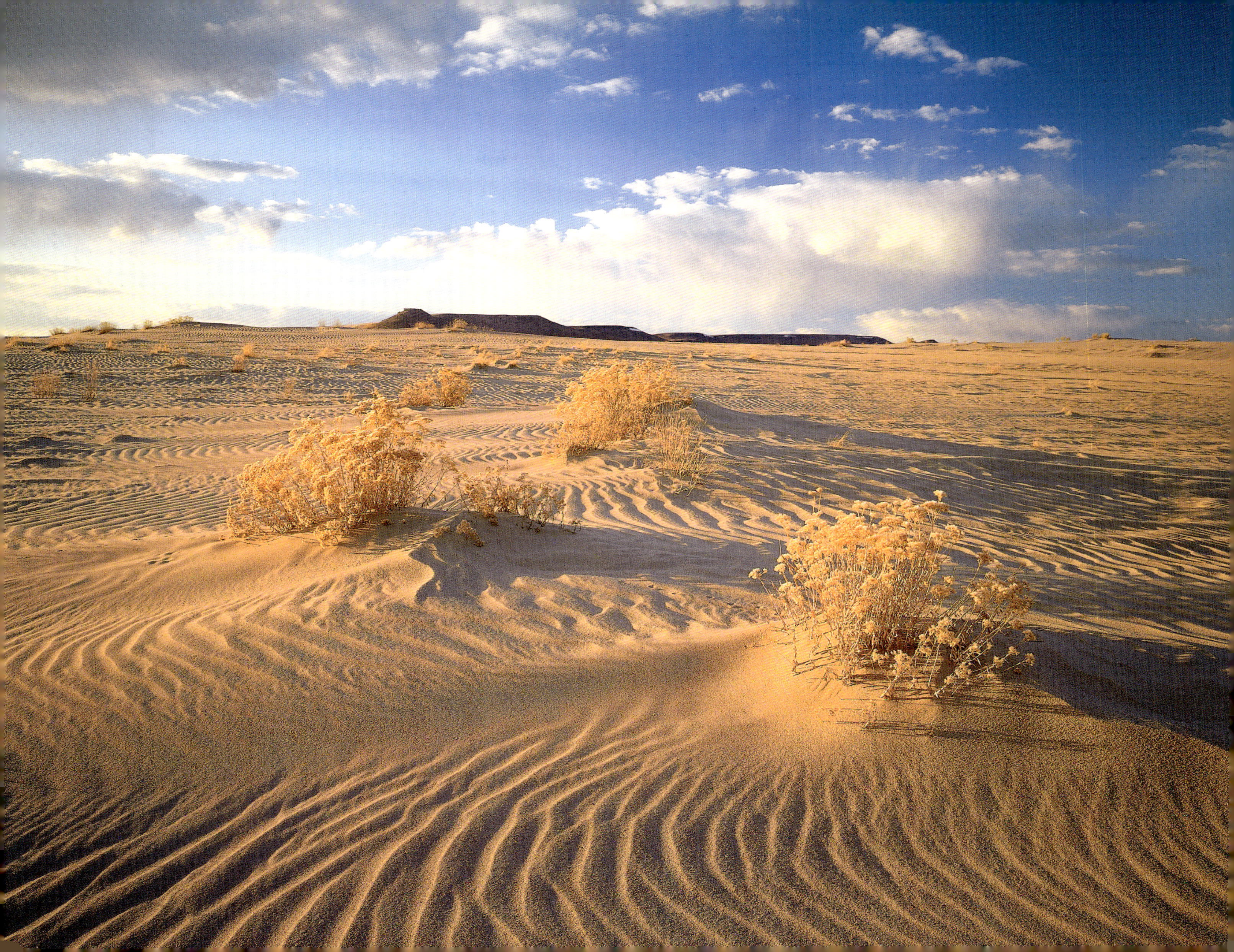

Foreword

The part of Wyoming traversed by the Continental Divide Trail was one of the last regions of the United States to be settled, and justifiably so. Gordon Jewett, with whom I built more miles of buck-and-rail fence than I care to recall, said that it was the last refuge of pioneers who couldn't get along with anyone, anywhere else. As the descendant of these cranks, he was worried: "I'm not happy," he said, "unless I'm pissed off."

That's about as encompassing a description of Wyoming character (and politics) as I can find. Humanity aside, this is still contrary, aggravating, expectation-squashing country. So why do I live here?

I sprang from Dissenters who fled from England after inciting violence, who then became Mormons and fled from the States after inciting more violence. Starting in 1847, my forebears crossed the Divide at South Pass on foot, on horseback, in wagons, dragging handcarts, to trouble the Shoshones and Utes. But the trails they followed, like most human tracks in the arid West, lay along the stream valleys: up the North Platte to its tributary, the Sweetwater, and then over the bright emptiness of South Pass to the Big Sandy River and the upper Green River.

In the Western interior, life tracks the course of water. That's one reason the Continental Divide Trail has so little historical precedent. And why, along much of its intended route, it doesn't exist except as an idea. Or perhaps it's closer to being an ideal: a geographic quest.

It's not an easy one. In Wyoming, the Divide behaves curiously indeed, leaving the peaks and snowfields, splitting for hundreds of miles around the wind-blasted sink of the Great Divide Basin, then looping west to bypass the noble bulk of Atlantic Peak on low ground. There, it stumbles along dry ridges and glittery outcrops above the Sweetwater River, which begins on the steep west face of the Wind River Range and seems to be bound not for the wide Missouri but for the Sea of Cortez: a puzzle as arresting as one of those Escher prints.

Frost blankets the grass and creek near Fish Creek Park in the Wind River Range. Mount Geikie is in the distance. Bridger Wilderness, Bridger-Teton National Forest.

I've known Scott Smith for years, first as an outdoor scruff and lately as one of the best outdoor photographers at work in the West. And though we've never shared a trip, I've spent considerable time along the route he depicts. For some reason, I never gazed on Old Faithful until 1992. But long before that, from a camp on the Buffalo Fork of the Snake River, I packed and guided for an outfitter in the Teton Wilderness. In July 1978, fording with a heavy pack, I was nearly flushed down Pole Creek in a roar of snowmelt. After that, I spent summers and falls in a tent below Union Pass, building log fences where three watersheds conjoin: Missouri, Columbia, and Colorado. In the 1980s, I patrolled grazing allotments in the Wind Rivers, dodged lightning bolts in the Sheep Desert, slept in a tiny cabin at Cross Lake, and drank coffee with a herder named Leandro (though, unlike the Leandro who Scott encountered, his last name was Duran and he came from Mexico).

Still later in my Forest Servitude, I spent seven years sampling wilderness rain and snow for airborne acids (risen from the ongoing industrial invasion of Wyoming). So I packed a small raft and science gear on llamas to lakes Scott mentions, and set up a snow collector on Lester Pass. In 1994, I helped with the first GPS survey of Knife Point Glacier, with hydrologist Craig Thompson and geologist Charlie Love of Western Wyoming College.

It's a life I love. Of course I took pictures—thousands. But they never looked this good. Scott Smith's photographs, painstakingly sought and beautifully reproduced, let me see places I know through bright new eyes.

Beauty, which this country has more of than food or warmth or money, is unforgiving. Beauty's too cold, too hot, too muddy, too dry, too windy, too buggy, too empty, all by semi-predictable turns. But, discovering a fossil fish miles from the nearest stream or camping under blue cirque walls on a glacial moraine, you sense the deeper pulse of change. Beauty does not forgive small-souled rules and five-year plans or welcome allotment and diversion. The best way to know it is not to hunker down and dig in, but like the pronghorn and bison and coyote, to stretch out and *go*.

Walking the Continental Divide through Wyoming is not just a physical risk. You might be disappointed, not just by circumstance but by how you face up to it. And over long stretches, with increasingly brutal development, it's not exactly a wilderness experience. So you might come home disturbed by the memory of "cowburnt" hills and blown-out streambeds damaged from overgrazing, or the craters and waste dumps left by mining, or the grid of roads and pipelines and pumpjacks—shrines to oil and gas. Even at night you might hear a drilling rig grinding away or see the dark plume of a coal-fired power plant across the moon.

Most people hike the wilderness parts and try to forget the rest. Given the various tricks that our species is up to these days, we're probably better off walking a trail someplace. And being somewhat abstract, a topographic jazz riff, the Continental Divide Trail matches our present time and mind.

Happiness doesn't follow rules. Like this country, it ebbs and flows—you take it as it comes, and grin, or end up with frostbite, nightmares, dust.

This is not the easiest way to go. That's why some of us will always try.

—C. L. Rawlins

C. L. Rawlins was born in Laramie, Wyoming, of Mormon-refugee parents. Educated at Utah State and Stanford universities, he joined the Forest Service in 1977. A firefighter, range rider, and field hydrologist, he won the USFS National Primitive Skills Award for measuring acid rain and snow in the Wind River Range. Concurrently, for 15 years, he was editor-at-large of Paonia, Colorado's, High Country News. *Upon leaving the Forest Service in 1992, his activist bent led him to serve on the board of the Greater Yellowstone Coalition and as president of the Wyoming Outdoor Council.*

While living the windblown life in Wyoming, presently in Laramie, Rawlins has written four books: A Ceremony on Bare Ground *(1985),* Sky's Witness: A Year in the Wind River Range *(1992),* Broken Country: Mountains and Memory *(1996), and* In Gravity National Park: Poems *(1998). At the moment he's working with Colin Fletcher to finish* The Complete Walker IV *(to be followed by a good, long walk).*

Introduction

*I*n late 1996, I had just finished a book called *Nevada: Magnificent Wilderness* for Westcliffe Publishers. Looking for a new book project, I approached Westcliffe with the idea of photographing the recently established Great Western Trail. Instead, the publisher asked if I would like to photograph the portion of the Continental Divide National Scenic Trail (CDNST) located in Wyoming.

Initially, they offered me the job of photographing for and writing the official guide to hiking Wyoming's portion of the trail, as well as providing photos for the volume you are holding. After brief consideration, I turned down the chance to pen the guide because I felt it would be impossible to do justice to the trail photographically *and* spend the time required to produce an accurate guidebook. My refusal of the guidebook writing opportunity made it possible for a *good* writer to do the job. Lora Davis hiked the entire trail through Wyoming. She took the meticulous notes, spent the hours over maps, and did the research necessary to produce an excellent guide. If any of the photos or stories in this book tempt you to hike the entire CDNST in Wyoming, or only a portion of it, I recommend you obtain a copy of Lora's book, *Wyoming's Continental Divide Trail: The Official Guide*. (Westcliffe publishes guides for the rest of the CDNST as well.)

In Wyoming, the CDNST traverses probably the most diverse terrain encountered along its entire route. A hiker passing through the conifer forests of the Sierra Madre, across the treeless and wind-abraded Great Divide Basin, along the lake-studded granite domes of the Wind River Range, and onto the steaming Yellowstone Plateau, encounters radical changes in elevation, geology, flora, and fauna.

Instead of through-hiking the CDNST, I entered and exited the route at various points during different times of the year in an attempt to capture each segment of the trail during its best season for photography. I took these photographs on 12 trips over a period of two years when I was shooting specifically for this book, and also during five other outings made previous to the book assignment when I was shooting for my stock file.

I felt no need to see every inch of the trail—I did explore about 430 miles of the 500-mile route—and had no intention of *hiking* all that I did travel. Many miles of the trail follow dirt, gravel, and even paved roads. It was much more efficient to drive heavy camera gear down those portions. I visited some segments more than once—sometimes on an out-and-back trip, sometimes returning to try again if my photographic efforts had been stymied previously by wind, rain, or heavily overcast skies. I did not limit my photos to only what one can see from the CDNST, but also photographed the Continental Divide itself, on occasions at some distance from the official trail.

After I had begun to photograph the Divide, the folks at Westcliffe asked me if I could write stories to accompany the images. Please keep in mind as you read this book that, although its layout follows the CDNST from south to north in a linear fashion, this is not the narrative of a purist start-at-the-beginning-hike-it-all-in-one-swoop backpacker. All of these stories and photographs are vignettes—words and images from the serial adventures of a photographer chasing the light along the Continental Divide Trail.

—*Scott T. Smith*

Squaretop Mountain reflects in the Green River. Bridger Wilderness, Wind River Range, Bridger-Teton National Forest.

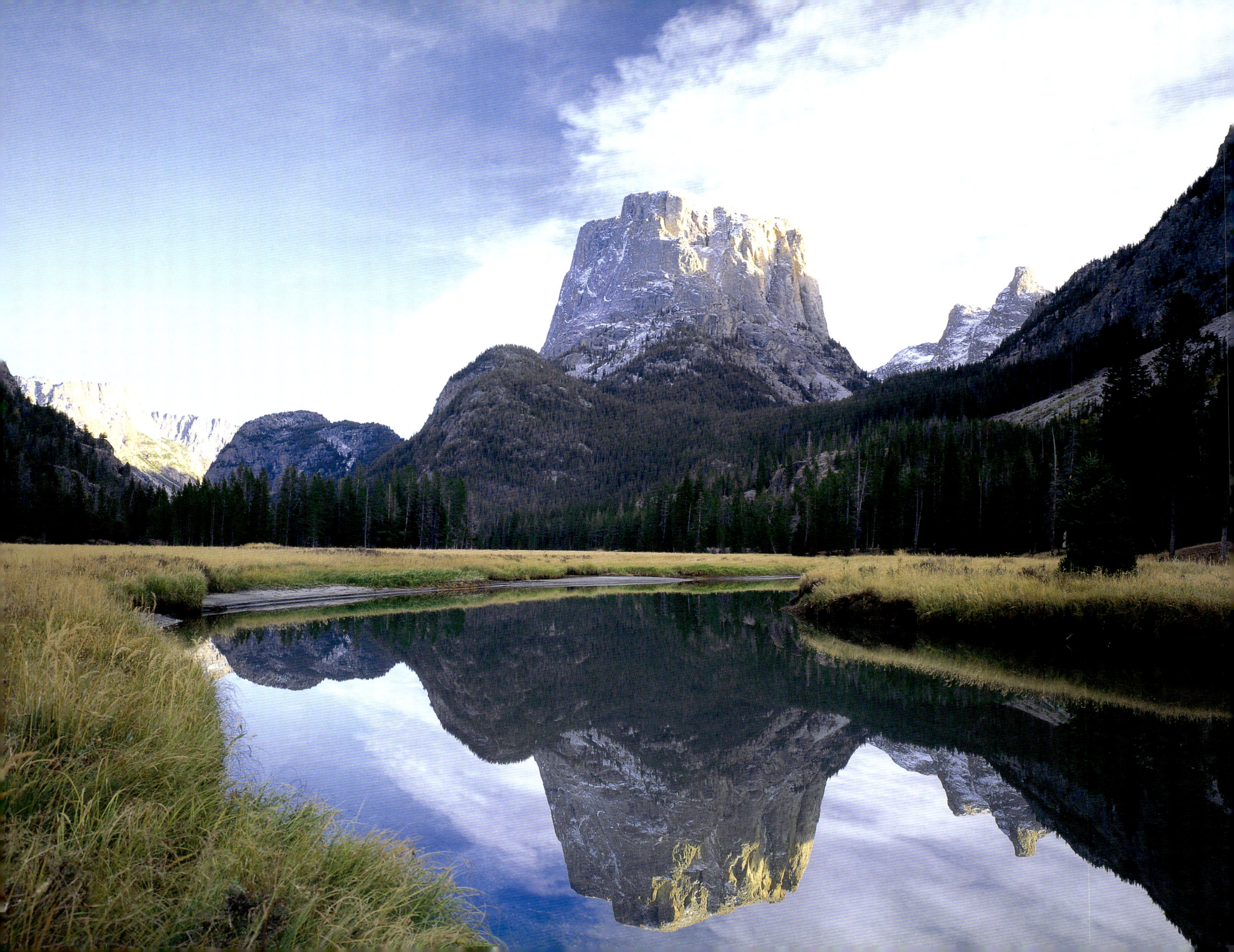

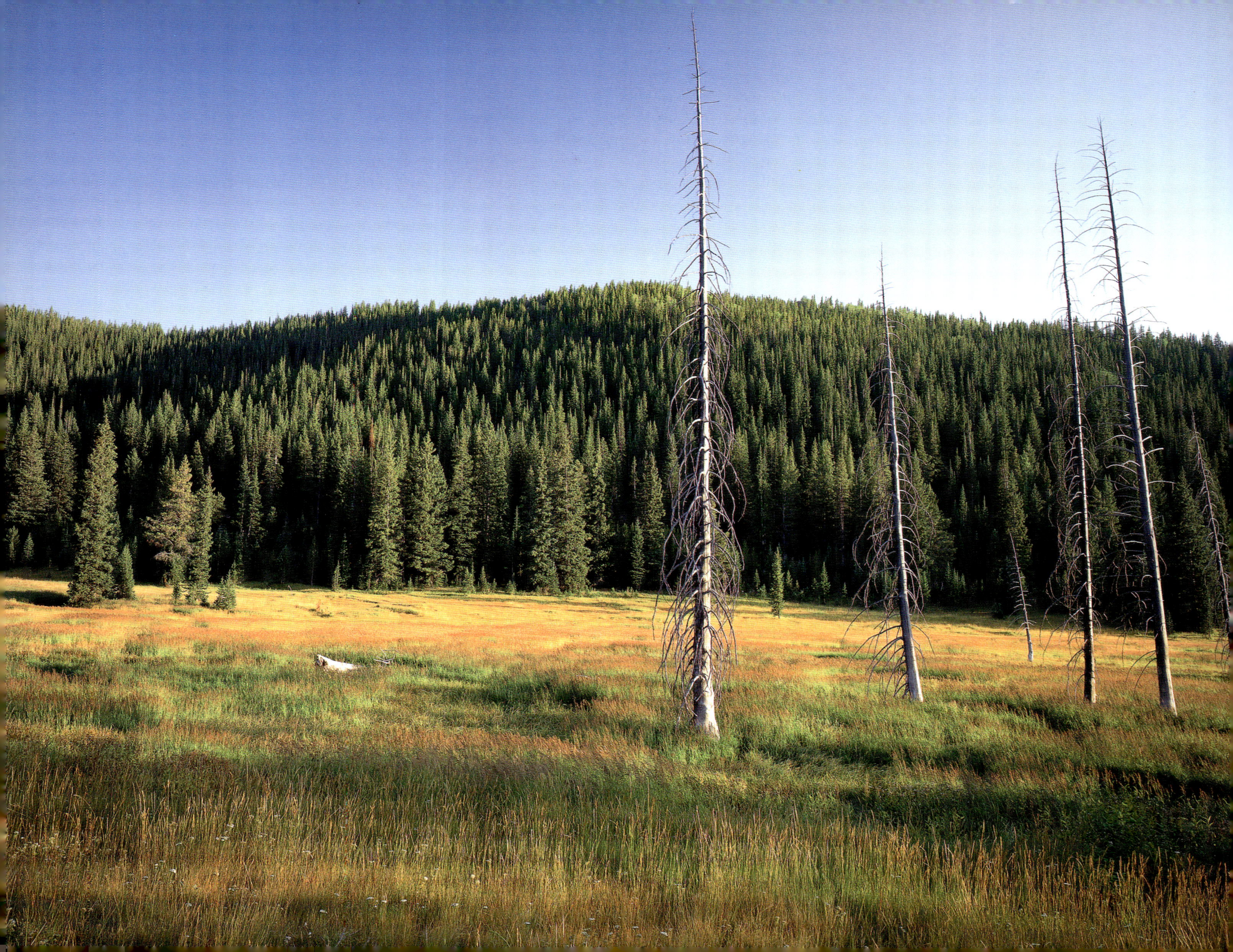

Sierra Madre

Huston Park Wilderness—September 1998

I have set up the camera in a gorgeous wet meadow in hopes that the sun will find a hole in the broken clouds before it sets in the west. In front of me are tall, green and gold grasses spiked with the silvery trunks of standing dead conifers. The forested ridge of the Continental Divide rises beyond. I am in the Huston Park Wilderness, but just barely. Behind me a ridiculously straight line of orange fiberglass markers indicates the official, though rather arbitrary looking, wilderness boundary. The last sign of humankind is a half-mile away at a dead-end road, and it seems to me the official wilderness should begin there. Nothing distinguishes the non-wilderness west end of the meadow from the officially wild remainder, save for the obtrusive orange markers. Clearly a line was ruled on a map in some office far from here with no regard to topography, vegetation, or anything else in the real world.

We noticed the same thing two days ago when we left Battle Pass. After following the Continental Divide Trail (CDT) along a forest road for a short distance, we passed the vehicles at the last hunters' camps, and headed off the Divide into a drainage disturbed by nothing but the trail. But it was another half-mile before we entered the Huston Park Wilderness. Wild country and wilderness boundary didn't coincide.

I am traveling with Scott Datwyler, a friend from Utah, and three of my pack llamas. Our goal this trip was to make a loop hike, partly along the southernmost portion of the CDT in Wyoming, and partly below the main ridge in the upper reaches of the Little Snake River drainage. Things went as planned for a day-and-a-half. Yesterday we walked through the "parks," the wonderful large meadows draped over the Divide, in late September still untouched by frost and dotted with wildflowers. We marveled at the views, and at the striking outcrops of red rocks that form the crest of the Sierra Madre here. This morning we headed down a little-maintained trail (nicely choked with deadfall) to the abandoned Verde Mine, just outside the Wilderness Area and above the West Branch North Fork Little Snake River. (Yes, that's the actual name. The lettering covers three miles on my topo map, the same distance we hiked this morning.)

We were propped against an enormous rusty boiler, eating lunch at the Verde Mine, when we heard a noise that shouldn't have been there:

A llama packer hikes the Continental Divide Trail in the Huston Park Wilderness. Sierra Madre, Medicine Bow National Forest.

Snags stand in a wet meadow below the Continental Divide. Huston Park Wilderness, Sierra Madre, Medicine Bow National Forest.

Spruce trees on the Continental Divide are silhouetted against the rising sun. Huston Park Wilderness, Sierra Madre, Medicine Bow National Forest.

"The last sign of humankind is a half-mile away at a dead-end road, and it seems to me the official wilderness should begin there."

the sound of a large diesel engine under load. Our map (photo-revised 1983) showed an old stock driveway we had planned to follow through the Little Snake drainage until we met the dead-end "Pipeline Road" not far below the Divide. Unfortunately the Pipeline Road was no longer a dead end and, sometime in the recent past, it had come to meet us, obliterating the stock trail in the process. Time to change the travel itinerary. After a cross-country traverse, a few miles on the graded gravel, and a little bushwhacking, we made it to this unspoiled meadow at the head of the North Fork. We decide to climb back to the Divide and the CDT tomorrow. The road-walking has shortened our loop, but we will still get to hike a number of miles on one of the few sections of the CDT located right on the Continental Divide.

In the meadow, the sun hasn't come out, and while I wait by the tripod, I reflect on the artificial lines we have imposed upon the land. An administrative line that cuts a wild meadow. Property lines. The perfect squares of township and range layered over the contours of my topographic maps. The arrow-straight border between Wyoming and Colorado just over the ridge. Not

Lichen-covered boulders pepper the Continental Divide. Huston Park Wilderness, Sierra Madre, Medicine Bow National Forest.

at all like the unambiguous natural feature of the Continental Divide, an irrefutable division of watersheds.

Then, with a flash, I realize that is not true of the Divide here. I understand what we were seeing as we walked along the Pipeline Road. Every creek and stream along the road enters a catchment structure, apparently entering the eponymous Pipeline. But the water does not stay on this side of the Divide. The road, the catchments, the pipeline: they are all part of a transbasin water diversion project. A tunnel must pierce the range, carrying water from the headwaters of the Little Snake River to the drainage of the North Platte. Water flowing through this meadow 60 years ago was beginning a journey down the Little Snake, Green, and Colorado rivers to the Gulf of California. Now it is rerouted to the Platte, Missouri, and Mississippi on its way to the Gulf of Mexico—if it makes it that far before being diverted again for irrigation, industrial use, a municipal water supply, or any of the myriad other demands made on Western water.

The sun breaks through and I take my photograph, chastened by our technological know-how and its effect on the integrity of the land.

Bridger Peak—June 1997

Today's goal is to photograph from the summit of Bridger Peak and to explore its surroundings. From Battle Pass, I can see an antenna on the summit, just now catching the light of sunrise. Also apparent is the rather large amount of snow lingering so late in the year—three days until the summer solstice. I park the truck 100 yards up the rough road to the summit. The road is also the CDT. I hope snow is blocking vehicle access along this route well below the peak. I want a day of solitude without the intrusive sounds and smells of gasoline engines.

I hoist "The Millstone," my 65-pound "daypack" containing large-format camera gear, film, and tripod, as well as water, lunch, extra clothes, headlamp, and first-aid kit, and trudge up the track between conifers and newly leafed aspen. Seven hundred feet below the summit, the road crosses to the north side of the ridge and, to my satisfaction, a six-foot drift lies at angles across it. After 30 more minutes of climbing snowfields and muddy patches of trail, I am examining the installation on Bridger Peak's rocky summit. At the base of the antenna is a room-sized metal box painted with a five-pointed star and "US ARMY," indicating military communications. It is emitting a faintly alarming whine so I move down the ridge a little way, just in case it is radiating super-secret microwaves that could mutate my DNA.

At just over 11,000 feet, Bridger Peak is the highest point along the CDT in southern Wyoming. For northbound hikers, the trail won't reach this elevation again until it traverses the Wind River Range, discernible as a

A sign marks the town of Encampment.

Wildflowers blossom in Huston Park Wilderness. Sierra Madre, Medicine Bow National Forest.

Metamorphic rock on the Continental Divide above the Little Snake River Drainage. Huston Park Wilderness, Sierra Madre, Medicine Bow National Forest.

pale bump on the horizon 150 miles away. The visibility today is amazing. The atmosphere is transparent. No haze limits my view, only the curvature of the Earth. To the south, the meadows on the crest of the Park Range unfurl below me. Colorado's Mount Zirkel looks close enough to walk to by sunset. The Little Snake River drainage encompasses Battle Mountain, as well as buttes many miles away where the Little Snake joins the Yampa. The Flat Tops, headwaters of the White River, are unmistakable; peering through binoculars, I can see peaks that are surely in Rocky Mountain National Park. I even convince myself that one is the distinctive pyramid of Longs Peak.

To the east, the bright white crest of the Snowy Range rises above the North Platte River Valley. To the north is a view I would find daunting if I were a CDT through-hiker. The land drops away to grassy ridges along the Continental Divide and the Atlantic Rim into the vast beige expanse of the Great Divide Basin. It is a long, treeless walk in the wind before the trail ascends the distant Wind River Mountains.

I snap a few photos, then drop off the peak and continue north on the CDT jeep track. Yesterday I started at Joe's Park, north of here, and hiked the CDT toward Bridger Peak. I want to walk far enough today to be able to see where I turned around yesterday. The trail traverses meadows and open forest for a couple miles along the gently sloping ridge that is the Continental Divide. North and South Spring Creek lakes glint below me in the upper

Battle Lake and Red Mountain viewed from the summit of Bridger Peak. Colorado's Mount Zirkel is visible in the distance. Sierra Madre, Medicine Bow National Forest.

Patches of snow are sprinkled along the Continental Divide below Bridger Peak. Sierra Madre, Medicine Bow National Forest.

reaches of the forested Jack Creek drainage. A number of clear-cut areas mar the slopes, reminding me that this is an extractive "multiple use" forest (it has been for more than a century). I am in the heart of the 100-year-old Grand Encampment Copper District. Just over the Divide to the west lie the remains of the Rudefeha Mine; in 1897, it was the richest strike in the district. Yesterday the CDT took me past shafts and ruined cabins at one of the numerous smaller mines that dot the Sierra Madre.

The trail begins to drop steeply and I stop. About two miles away I can see the place on the open ridge above Jack Creek where I retreated yesterday. I was surprised to find a garden of cactus there, growing at 9,300 feet in elevation right on the Continental Divide. I am only 1,300 feet higher here, but in a very different life zone, standing on a drift of June snow that is melting into a dark conifer forest.

Back on the slope just below Bridger Peak, I put the camera away but am reluctant to begin hiking back to the truck. The day is still dazzlingly clear and the late afternoon sun is warm here out of the wind, so I decide to stay for a while. Beginning to doze, I am roused by a bark behind me. A cow elk has come over the ridge. She senses my presence but can't find me as I remain crouched, motionless, behind the log that was recently my pillow. She wants to continue across the slope, but the snow and scree below the peak, as well as the log I am hiding behind, impede her preferred route. Ears cocked, her nostrils flare as she tries to pinpoint the

Wildflowers and aspen sway in the wind on the Continental Divide near Joe's Park. Sierra Madre, Medicine Bow National Forest.

Lupine blooms along the Continental Divide. Sierra Madre, Medicine Bow National Forest.

> *"I was surprised to find a garden of cactus there, growing at 9,300 feet right on the Continental Divide."*

danger she senses. Uncertain, she barks again and gives up for now, silently backtracking over the rise and just out of sight. She barks at intervals, a weird, high-pitched, short exhalation that sounds much like the finishing note of a bull elk's bugle. Twice she comes back to the bottleneck before she braves the dash. Her eyes roll white as she passes within 40 feet of me. Once beyond the perceived danger, she slows her gallop to a trot and glides into the forest.

At dusk, on the way down, I see more elk tracks embedded in the snow, as well as those of a four-wheel-drive vehicle that churned up the wet hillside as it muscled around several of the snowdrifts. I am glad I walked.

■ ■ ■

Wildflowers and cacti on the Continental Divide. Sierra Madre, Medicine Bow National Forest.

A cumulonimbus cloud launches a violent thunderstorm over the rangeland below the Sierra Madre.

Jim Bridger

His name is all over the maps of Wyoming. Along the Continental Divide, you will find Bridger Peak, Bridger Pass, Bridger Wilderness, and Bridger National Forest. Nearby are Fort Bridger, Bridger Lake, and even Bridger Power Plant.

Jim Bridger is perhaps the most famous of the legendary mountain men. One of the first whites to use the Indian trail over South Pass, he is credited with discovering the Great Salt Lake. He ran the Bighorn River rapids in a raft, selected the route of the Overland Stage Trail through Bridger Pass, and pioneered trails through the Laramie Mountains and the Bighorn Basin.

For many years, Bridger resided with one Indian tribe or another and came to share many of their ways. He could reportedly tell a story in complete silence by using only Indian sign language, keeping his audience enthralled as they laughed at his humor or cried out in amazement.

Famous for his tall tales, and foremost in describing the Yellowstone region, he told stories of fish swimming over mountains, boiling pools suddenly leaping into the sky, and forests made of stone—and they were not believed. But anyone who has seen Two Ocean Creek split on the Continental Divide, watched Great Fountain Geyser erupt, or walked among the petrified trees on Specimen Ridge knows that Jim Bridger may have embellished the truth, but he certainly wasn't lying.

PHOTO FROM THE DENVER PUBLIC LIBRARY WESTERN HISTORY DEPARTMENT

Stormy skies clear with the coming of sunset over the slopes of the Sierra Madre. Medicine Bow National Forest.

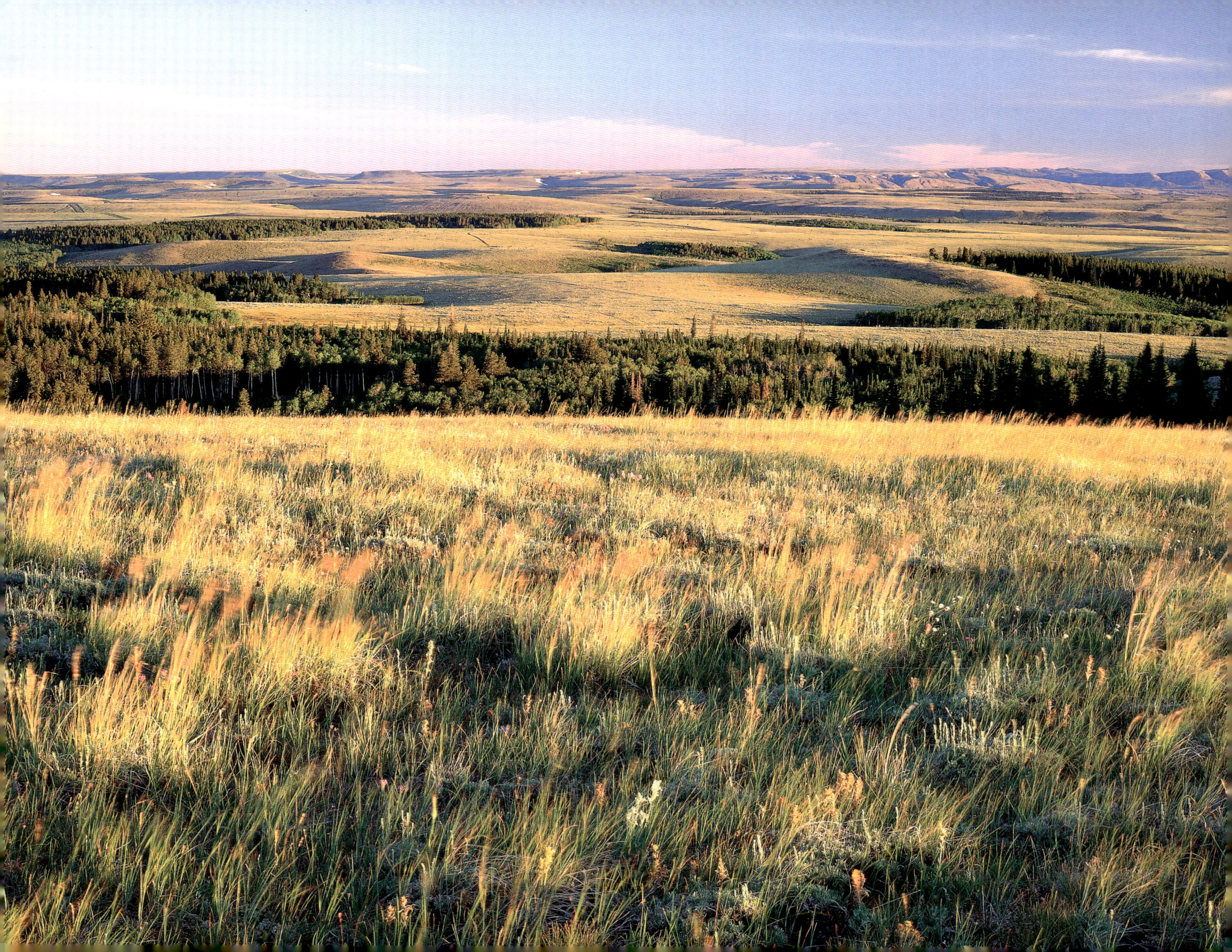

Great Divide Basin

Atlantic Rim—June 1997

My truck shudders in the gusts as grit lifted from the jeep track sandblasts the driver's side. It's just a typical afternoon in the wind tunnel of south-central Wyoming. Well, maybe it is blowing a bit harder than usual. The outflow from a towering cumulonimbus cloud—flickering with lightning and dragging a black curtain of rain out of the west—augments the nearly perpetual wind. I am parked on the Atlantic Rim above Bridger Pass, exposed to the full fury of the blast. Things are about to get wet. I would like to move to a more protected spot, but the truck has a flat tire. It is not long until sunset and I don't want to try to put the spare on now in the wind and rain, or later in the mud and dark, so I roll out my mummy bag in the pickup bed and camp here under the shell. Maybe the wind will rock me to sleep.

Thunder booms as big, high-velocity raindrops begin to pelt the truck, sounding more like thrown pebbles than something liquid. I flinch as lightning hits the ridge much too close to where I am sitting. I reached the shelter of the vehicle just in time.

A two-track dirt road winds across the Great Divide Basin.

I spent the afternoon walking along the escarpment of the Atlantic Rim, the hydrologic divide between the Platte River and…no other river at all, but a closed basin. At Bridger Pass, the Continental Divide splits in two: Atlantic and Pacific rims. The two arms of the Divide rejoin many miles away at South Pass, and between them they cradle the Great Divide Basin, 3,500 square miles of dunes, seasonal alkaline lakes, and arid hills. Precipitation that falls within its boundaries sinks into the ground or evaporates. If downpours like the one now filling the gullies and arroyos around me with muddy runoff were frequent, there would likely be a large lake in the Great Divide Basin. But the region receives only seven inches of precipitation annually. It is a harsh, dry, unforgiving place, but one of severe beauty. I love deserts, but right now I am glad not to be a through-hiker on the Continental Divide Trail (CDT) worried about the logistics of crossing the Great Divide Basin on foot.

There is no actual CDT on the ground here or even, as of June 1997, an official route across the Great Divide Basin. I view it as more of a wide CDT corridor where you look at maps, weigh your alternatives, and roll

Grassland and forest mark this portion of the Continental Divide, as viewed from Joe's Park near the Atlantic Rim.

Pond and alkali on Emigrant Creek below Bridger Pass.

your own trail. Between here and Rawlins, located on Interstate 80 near the railroad, and for 20 miles north of Rawlins, there are not many routing options for the CDT, and all of them follow graded and paved roads. This difficulty arises from private land conflicts caused by "The Checkerboard." When the transcontinental railroad was being constructed 130 years ago, the U.S. government offered an incentive to the Union Pacific Railroad—it gave every other section of land to the railroad for 20 miles north and south of the tracks. This checkerboard pattern of alternating one-mile-square parcels of private and public land still exists, making it problematic to locate the CDT anywhere but along a road right-of-way.

I drove from Rawlins several days ago, exploring this part of the Continental Divide by vehicle and by foot. The storm and flat tire have kept me from driving back tonight. Except for a brief respite at dawn at Little Sage Reservoir, I have been battling the wind to make photos—not just because the vegetation waves wildly, but because the whole camera and tripod shake. At ephemeral Five Mile Lake, June snowbanks melting on the lee side of the Atlantic Rim fed a broad expanse of shallow water. I tried to walk to the water's edge across the ostensibly solid alkaline crust surrounding the lake but, still a long way from the shore, broke through and sank ankle-deep into mud. The muck beneath the surface was weirdly warm, the crust and underlying moisture somehow concentrating solar energy.

A sign along the Continental Divide Trail identifies private land within "The Checkerboard" of land ownership south of Rawlins.

Hiking along the Atlantic Rim this afternoon, I saw some real Wyoming cowboys. I could tell they were working cowboys by the cut of their clothes—no Western fashion statement here, just something to keep them warm while they paid attention to moving the cows and calves. Only one had a cowboy hat, a beat-up straw one. Another sported an engineer's cap, and the last a greasy baseball cap advertising a taxidermist in Saratoga. There was not a snakeskin boot in sight. All three wore worn work boots, and stained and torn coveralls. Functional apparel for dirty work.

One of the cowboys rode over to talk. My Spanish was about as good as his English, so we mostly gestured and smiled. I tried to explain why I was walking around in the desert with a big pack on. I pantomimed snapping a photo and tried the words "camera" and "*un fotógrafo*." He shook his head (in disbelief or incomprehension) and then pointed to the rapidly building cumulus clouds in the west. I caught "raining" and "*relámpago*" as he turned his horse and cantered after his mates and the cattle as they hustled off the ridge.

Sandstone on the Atlantic Rim along the Continental Divide.

The rain stops at dusk and the hem of the clearing clouds glows red. I think about trying for a photo, but when I get out of the truck and lean into the sustained 40-mile-per-hour wind, I decide I might not be able to keep the tripod upright, let alone hold it steady.

By dawn the wind has slackened enough so none of the landscape is airborne. The all-night gale has dried the ground. I soon change the tire and am on my way down the CDT at a good clip, headed for Rawlins, a tire patch, and breakfast.

"The outflow from a towering cumulonimbus cloud—flickering with lightning and dragging a black curtain of rain out of the west—augments the nearly perpetual wind."

Ferris Dunes—May 1997

The sand that makes up the Ferris Dunes pours like fine sugar through my hands. The individual grains are all nearly the same size, well-rounded, and a translucent gold. Round grains typify sand that has traveled a long distance, with edges worn away on the journey. This sand originated in the Green River Basin and has been blown across the entire Great Divide Basin by the persistent west wind.

I have been exploring possible CDT routes through the Great Divide Basin with writer Lora Davis. Lora is writing the guidebook

Atlantic Rim and Little Sage Reservoir at sunrise.

Conifers sway gently in the wind at the Nine Mile Hill pine grove.

to the Wyoming portion of the CDT, and she will walk across most of the basin in the near future. But for now, we use my four-wheel-drive truck to explore a few of the numerous dirt roads and two-track jeep trails that crisscross the desert.

This is our last camp before I take Lora back to her car at Bairoil, and I am pleased the wind that has roared out of the west for the last few days is finally relenting enough so I can set up my large-format camera. The sun is nicely cross-lighting the rippled dunes piled below the steep south face of the Ferris Mountains, and I would like to get some shots before it sets.

I left Lora back at the truck and hiked a couple miles into the highest dunes while she made notes on her maps and in her journal. From a dune's crest I can see how the wind has piled the sand against the barriers of the Ferris and Seminoe mountains, and how some of the sand blows over the eastern arm of the Continental Divide, past Bear Mountain, and on toward Pathfinder Reservoir on the Platte River. A hundred miles away, on the opposite side of the Great Divide Basin, the western arm of the Continental Divide presents a similar barrier at Steamboat Mountain. The Killpecker Dunes collect at its base. Between the Killpecker Dunes and the Ferris Dunes, a long crescent of sand—marching dunes that I have seen from the window of an airliner—migrates east.

Writer Lora Davis decides not to drink the water. Crooks Gap Road, Great Divide Basin.

Only a light breeze accompanies the sunset, so I make some photos. I love to photograph dunes. They have a rhythm and softness, a sort of femininity that is pleasing to the human eye. The intertwining ripples on the surface of the dunes and the smooth S-curves of their crests contrast with the hard angles of the Ferris Mountains rising behind them.

As I walk back in the failing light, a cottontail is disturbed by my passing. The animal leaves distinctive prints in the sand when it scampers to the cover of a rabbitbrush. I am looking forward to exploring the dunes at dawn. With no wind to cover tracks, the sand will act as a register of nocturnal comings and goings.

Sand dunes in the American West teem with wildlife because they support a greater diversity of plants than the surrounding desert. Dunes are something of an oasis because they hold more available moisture than the adjacent alkali and clay. The dunes in the Great Divide Basin are particularly effective in holding water because of a phenomenon called "Aeolian ice lenses." During winter storms, snowdrifts form on the lee side of dunes. Then sand blows and covers the snow, trapping and insulating it within the dune. In the spring and early summer, this reservoir slowly melts, sustaining a surprisingly diverse population of plants and animals.

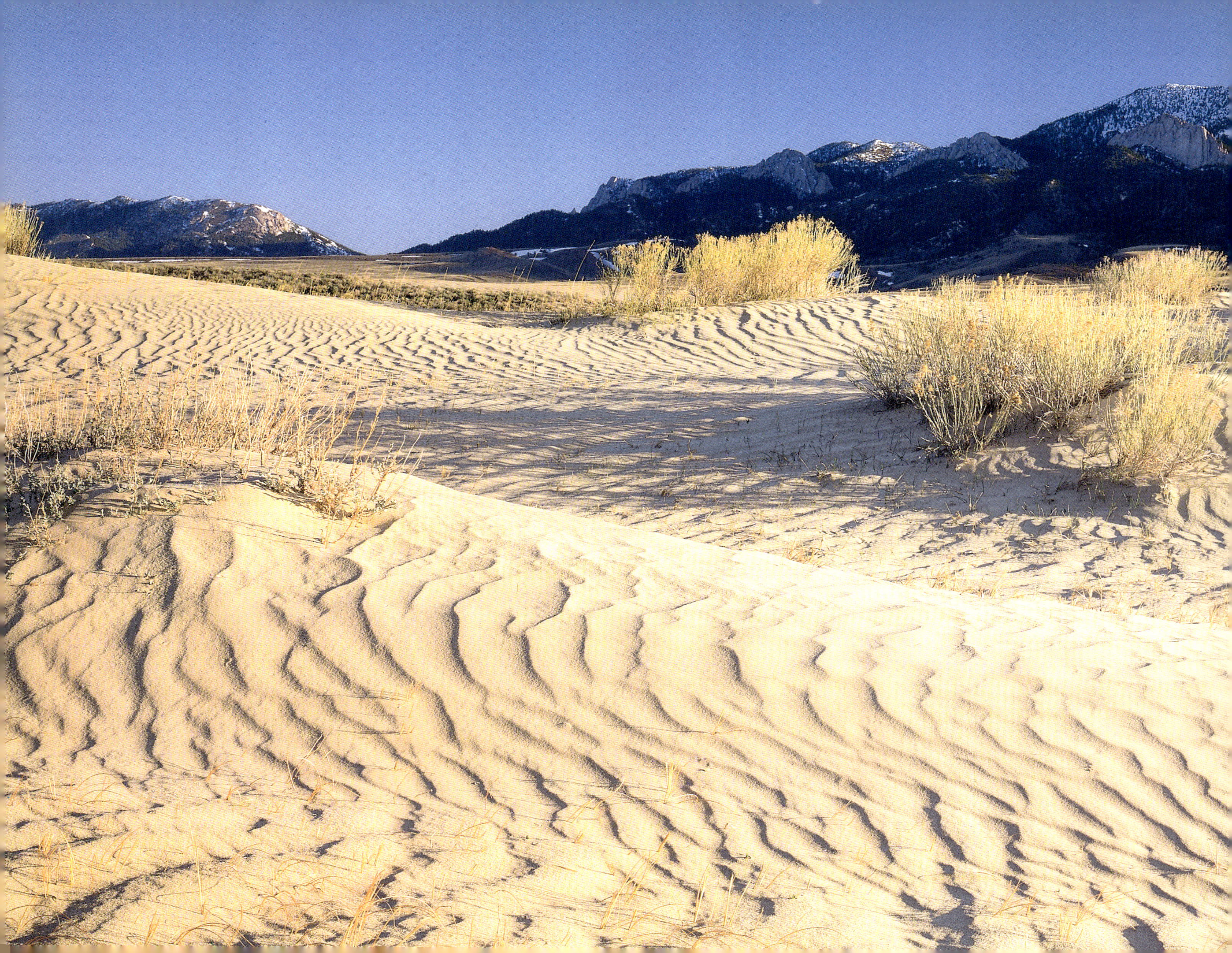

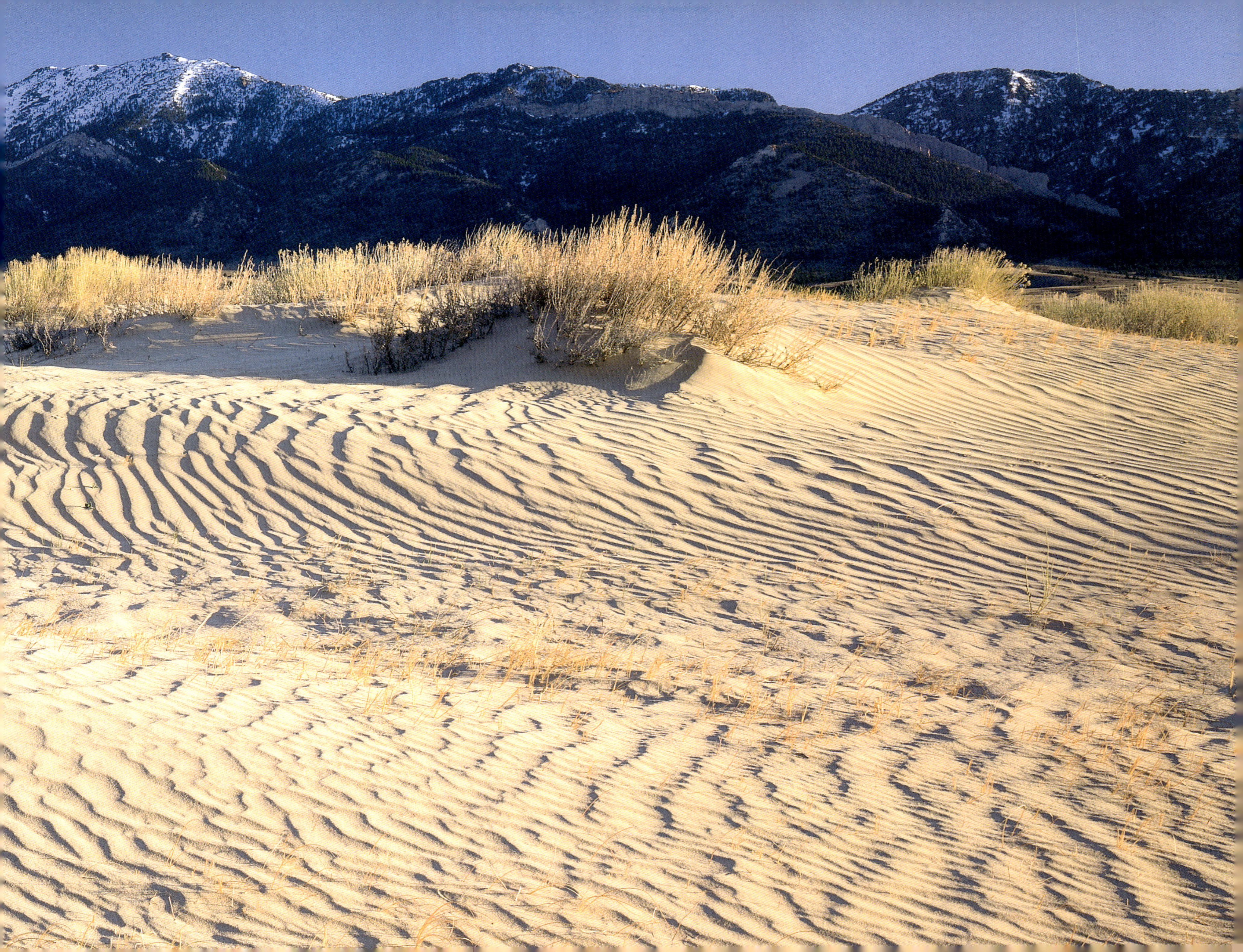

American pronghorns roam the Great Divide Basin. The Wind River Range looms in the distance.

A herd of wild horses near Cyclone Rim and the head of Alkali Creek.
Previous page: Rabbitbrush grows on the Ferris Dunes below the Ferris Mountains.

Several years ago, my wife, Mary, and I camped one night in the Killpecker Dunes in early spring. Not only was there moisture in the sand, but there were ponds between the dunes. It was remarkable to see a desert landscape mirrored in water, and even more wondrous to lie on a dune in our sleeping bags and hear the calls of sandhill cranes and the murmurings of fitful geese roosting on the ponds.

Mary and I ventured out on the Killpecker Dunes at dawn, trying to decipher the record of the night's activity. A maze of tracks told us that beetles and mice had zigzagged across the sand. Cottontails and jackrabbits had moved from bush to bush between the dunes, sometimes tentatively, sometimes making long bounds. A telltale line of prints was made by webbed feet—geese walking from one pond to another.

Shortly after sunrise, we came upon a line of coyote tracks and holes dug in damp sand. Closer examination revealed the coyote was digging for grubs, probably beetle larvae. We followed the meandering tracks over one dune crest, then another. Mary observed that the digging looked fresher; maybe the coyote was still out and just ahead of us. We crept to the next crest and there he was below us, nose to the sand and digging a shallow pit. The coyote was instantly aware of us, in full flight, and out of sight over the adjacent dune in seconds. In a moment we saw it again, cresting a distant dune, still at top speed, never looking back. An experienced animal. Coyotes that stop within rifle range in this part of the world don't live to do it many times.

The wind rose as we backtracked along the coyote's trail, and sand began to fill the tracks, erasing evidence of its passage, creating a blank page on which another story could be written.

Lichen-covered rock outcrop in the Great Divide Basin. Bull Springs Rim is visible in the distance.

Boulders and limber pines along the Continental Divide on Crooks Mountain.

Lichen on rock above the Sweetwater River.

"I love photographing dunes. They have a rhythm and softness, a sort of femininity that is pleasing to the human eye."

The Boar's Tusk punctuates the landscape at the Killpecker Dunes Wilderness Study Area.

South Pass

At an elevation of 7,550 feet, South Pass is not a dramatic notch in the Continental Divide, but rather an almost imperceptible saddle on a gradually sloping high plain, 20 miles wide. Between 1824 and the coming of the Union Pacific Railroad, hundreds of thousands of emigrants crossed South Pass on their way to the West. In 1812, Robert Stuart and a party of Astorians returning from Oregon were the first whites to navigate the pass. They did not publicize their discovery, and the route remained unknown until 1824 when Crow Indians told Jedediah Smith and a party of trappers about an easy route over the Continental Divide south of the Wind River Mountains.

Mountain men used South Pass extensively, and in 1841 the first of a stream of emigrant wagon trains rolled through. The major migration routes, the Oregon, California, and Mormon trails, all surmounted the Continental Divide at South Pass.

Today, South Pass looks much the same as it did to emigrants a century-and-a-half ago. No railroad or highway was ever built through the pass, and the once busy thoroughfare is marked only by primitive dirt roads and historic wagon ruts.

■ ■ ■

Historic mining ruins near South Pass City.

Grasses and sagebrush flourish on the Continental Divide near South Pass. Oregon Buttes rise in the distance.

Wind-twisted limber pines cling to a bluff above the Sweetwater River near South Pass.

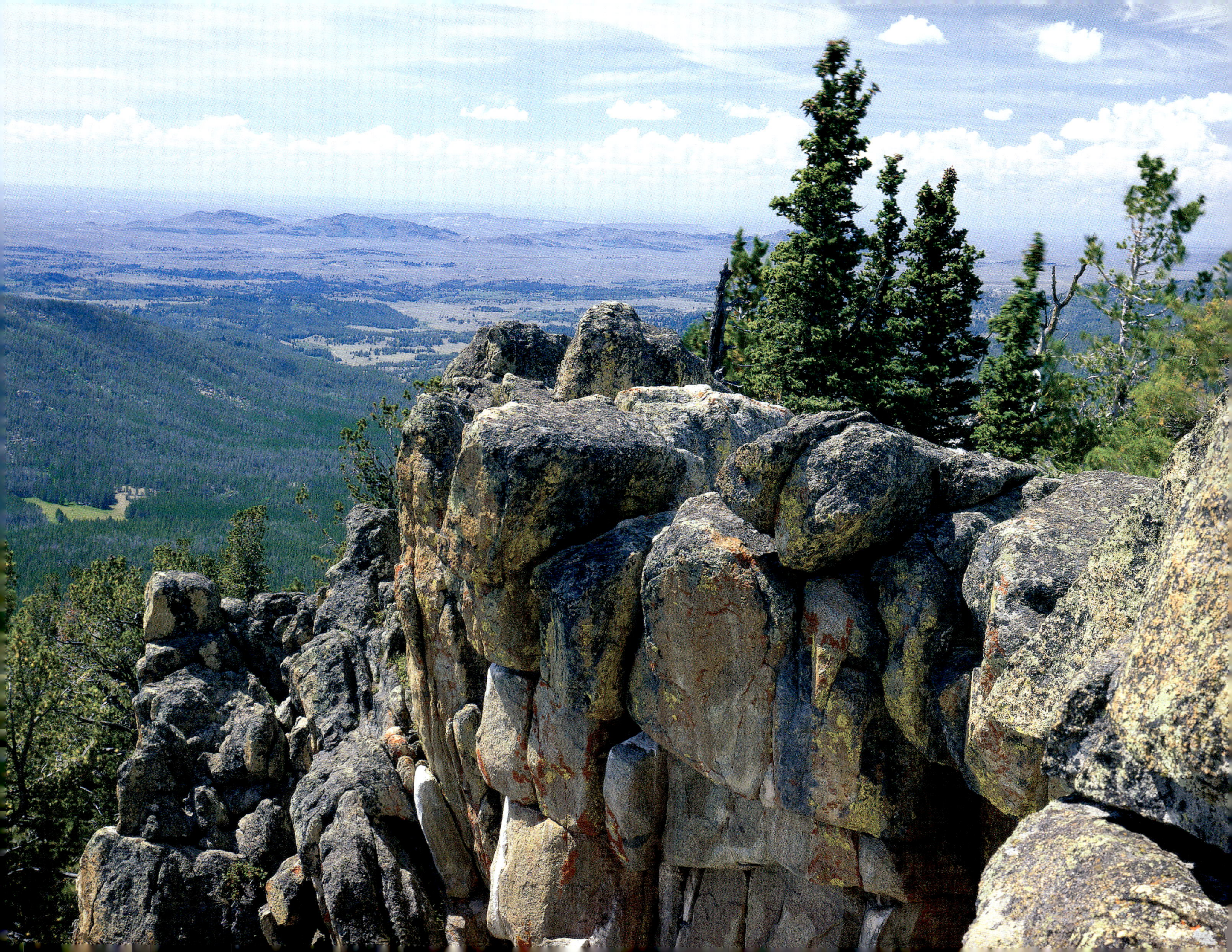

Wind River Range

Cross Lake—July 1997

The young weasels dart about the rocks like corn popping or a demonstration in Brownian Motion. I think there are seven, but it is hard to tell. They bounce around the landscape so rapidly it seems like twice that number.

I have my large-format camera set up on a slope above the meadow containing Cross and Raid lakes. Meadow is an inadequate description. It is a miles-long, nearly treeless park of short grass located on an almost flat bench at 10,000 feet. Across the park to the east, on the other side of Cross Lake, the Continental Divide Trail (CDT) winds below the sawtooth summits of Dragonhead Peak, Pronghorn Peak, and Mount Bonneville.

I had been waiting for the sun to drop below the hem of the clouds to the west and illuminate the lakes and mountains with warm, photographically pleasing light, when an adult short-tailed weasel appeared with a mouse in its mouth. She (I assume it was mom) dropped the mouse near a truck-sized boulder and left. Shortly after, juvenile weasels began erupting from the crevices beneath the boulder.

Wild strawberries can be picked near Upper Green River Lake. Bridger Wilderness, Wind River Range, Bridger-Teton National Forest.

The tiny weasels are beautiful, only four or five inches long with smooth brown coats and eyes like bright black beads. Completely fearless, they come right up to my boots and stop for a second or two, checking me out before dashing off again. One even grabs my laces and shows every intention of climbing my trouser leg before I move (jump, really) and scare it away. All the while, they are making an indescribable sound—sort of a purring burble or a chirpy hum. They seem to be having a great time. As they race about, sometimes two will meet and initiate a short, frantic wrestling match. One occasionally races over to the mouse the adult left and shakes it vigorously before flinging it away. It is amazing how quick they are and how small an opening they can squeeze through. They zoom over, around, and under the broken rocks on the slope, negotiating tiny cracks at full speed. I notice that, for all their energy, they remain close, never venturing more than about 30 feet from their den under the boulder.

Mary is just over the ridge, back at camp with the llamas, and I feel a little guilty that I am getting to

Little Sweetwater River drainage viewed from the summit of Granite Peak. Wind River Range, Shoshone National Forest.

see these fascinating animals and she is not. But she is out of shouting range, and I am afraid that if I leave to get her, they may be gone by the time we return. Unfortunately, I am unable to take any photos of the weasels—I have only my large-format view camera with me, and it is too cumbersome to capture these frenetic creatures on film.

I have been so engrossed that I haven't noticed the sun has dropped below the clouds and is about to set. I have missed the best light, but still shoot a few exposures. By the time I pack up my gear, dusk is falling. The youngsters still play as I hoist the pack and start up toward camp.

> *"The young weasels dart about the rocks like corn popping or a demonstration in Brownian Motion."*

We are on an out-and-back hike in the southern Wind River Range. Eight days ago we started at Big Sandy Opening, getting as far as Victor Lake below Hat Pass before turning around. We have taken a detour off the CDT on the way back, making camp on a ridge between Cross Lake and Upper Silver Lakes in an attempt to catch a breeze and get some relief from the voracious mosquitoes.

Not far away lies the infamous "Sheep Desert," a badly overgrazed area where every band of sheep stops to rest and feed

Aspen in autumn near the East Fork Little Sweetwater River. Wind River Range, Bridger-Teton National Forest.

Aspen and sagebrush thrive on the Continental Divide in the foothills of the Wind River Range. The Prospect Mountains are visible in the distance.

A whitebark pine at sunrise. Bridger Wilderness, Wind River Range, Bridger-Teton National Forest.

after being driven out of a steep canyon. We haven't seen any egregious grazing damage, but we have seen sheep. Thousands of sheep. We dodged three bands of 400 to 500 each, being driven toward Raid Lake. On a promontory just below us, a large, canvas tent belonging to herders of a fourth band occupies the breeziest camp spot. We can hear the bleating of their animals, gathered nearby for the night.

At sunrise, Mary and I travel back to what we have dubbed "Weasel Rock." There is no sign of the critters as I set up for morning photos of Cross and Raid lakes. About the time I am ready to shoot, Mary notices the sheep that had been crowded together last night are now dispersing to graze—and heading up the slope to where the llamas are tethered. Sheep alone approaching the llamas probably wouldn't cause a problem, but the Great Pyrenees guard dogs that move with the sheep, and the active smaller shepherd dogs, are a different matter. Mary starts back at a trot. I take several quick shots, then hastily pack up the gear, listening for sounds of barking or shouts for help.

With some apprehension, I round the outcrop that hides our camp and find that the sheep and their accompanying canines have been driven back down the hill. The llamas (and Mary) are calm, and are being studied by a Peruvian herder named Leandro on a large roan horse. We invite him to have coffee with us and visit for a while.

Hikers camp near Dads Lake. Bridger Wilderness, Wind River Range, Bridger-Teton National Forest.

Even though Leandro is from Peru, where llamas are native, he has never seen them up close and is curious about how we pack them and how much they cost. He has been working in the United States for eight years, tending sheep for various outfits in Idaho and Wyoming, the last two years here in the Winds. When we ask him how he is treated, he tells us his current employer keeps him well-supplied and provides good horses and equipment. Past employers were not so conscientious. He does not make much money by U.S. standards, but more than he could in South America. He sends most of his earnings back to his family in Peru. We inquire about all the sheep we saw yesterday. "Are they all from the same ranch you work for?" He says no, there are several grazing permitees here—too many, he thinks. He is concerned that the individual bands are too big to

A grassy tarn below Medina Mountain at sunset. Bridger Wilderness, Wind River Range, Bridger-Teton National Forest.

WIND RIVER RANGE 49

Cross and Raid lakes below the Continental Divide. Bridger Wilderness, Wind River Range, Bridger-Teton National Forest.

Author Lora Davis loads her pack llama.

manage properly and that there are too many sheep chasing too little forage in this high country.

Leandro mounts up to tend his flock and we wish him good luck for the rest of his summer in the mountains. He will stay here until September; we will leave this part of the range in two days. Later, as we lead the llamas down toward Cross Lake and the CDT, I look back up at Weasel Rock and think I detect motion at its base. I mentally wish the weasels good luck during their stay in the mountains as well.

Pole Creek—July 1998

Pole Creek was knee-deep, swift and cold, but the water was low enough to get ourselves and the llamas across this morning—the only casualty my blackened toenail. I obtained

Middle Fork Boulder Creek flows through the Wind River Range. Bridger Wilderness, Bridger-Teton National Forest.

A large boulder protrudes from the shore of Victor Lake below North Fork Peak. Bridger Wilderness, Wind River Range, Bridger-Teton National Forest.

this injury when Rocket, the llama at the head of the string I was leading across the creek, tried to pass and bumped me with a pannier. I stumbled and my sandal-clad foot struck a submerged rock. It hurt like crazy and a few colorful words flew in Rocket's direction. I thought Pole Creek Crossing was going to be the crux of this trip, but we have just been informed that snow may still block a pass along our route.

Shanna and Doug, my sister and her husband, have joined Mary and me for a llama trek along the CDT in the northern Wind River Range. Carrying our gear are my llamas Rocket, Poncho, and Cronus. We started our hike yesterday at Elkhart Park and hope to continue up Pole Creek until we meet the CDT and follow it over Lester Pass. From there we'll travel through the upper Fremont Creek and Elbow Creek drainages, then down the Green River to Green River Lakes. We will traverse more than 40 miles of some of the most spectacular terrain in the Rocky Mountains, passing below the highest peaks in Wyoming and through the long, U-shaped valley of the upper Green River.

Last summer, Mary and I also began at Elkhart Park, but took a shorter route to meet the CDT. We did not have to cross Pole Creek or negotiate Lester Pass. We got as far as Elbow Lake before backtracking. Though we don't want to, we may have to backtrack on this trip as well. At 11,100 feet, Lester Pass is the highest elevation the CDT reaches in Wyoming, and the south

Asters sprout through a crack in the glacier-polished granite along Pole Creek. Bridger Wilderness, Wind River Range, Bridger-Teton National Forest.

The Continental Divide Trail at Lester Pass. Bridger Wilderness, Wind River Range, Bridger-Teton National Forest.

A llama packer treks across Lester Pass. Bridger Wilderness, Wind River Range, Bridger-Teton National Forest.

side of the pass can hold a snowfield with a nearly vertical cornice well into summer. I had called the Forest Service before we drove to the trailhead and asked if Lester Pass had melted out enough to get pack stock through. A staffer assured me the pass was open. But shortly after crossing Pole Creek, we met a wilderness ranger who had been at Lester Pass five days ago. He did not dare attempt the cornice carrying a heavy pack. If the pass is blocked, we will be forced to use the Elkhart to Titcomb Basin Trail, the most heavily used trail in the Wind River Mountains. On our way back to Elkhart last summer, Mary and I encountered 132 people along a five-mile stretch of the trail, a wilderness traffic jam I don't want to experience again.

The days have been very warm and the snow is melting fast. If the pass has opened, we may see backpackers on the trail. Not wanting to make a decision about turning around yet, we decide to continue to Cook Lakes and spend the night. The Upper and Lower Cook Lakes are part of a classic glacial landscape: large, deep-blue gems set in ice-scoured granite. The Continental Divide rises above the basin, a skyline of nearly 13,000-foot peaks flashing in the sun.

In the morning, I notice a rather ragtag and muddy group of backpackers on the trail—Boy Scouts on a "Forty-Miler." The scouts seem energetic enough, though not particularly happy, but the adult troop leaders (trailing a good distance behind the boys) seem a bit worse for wear. Judging by their ample bellies and flushed faces, I suspect they may not have gotten into optimum physical condition before heading out to carry 60-pound loads to 11,000 feet. They have come over Lester Pass. One of the leaders says the cornice has melted back and there are only about 50 yards of snow to cross. I ask one of the youngsters if it was scary. "Naw, we're mountaineers!"

Cumulus clouds form above the Teton Range at sunset, viewed from the Continental Divide near Union Pass. Bridger-Teton National Forest.

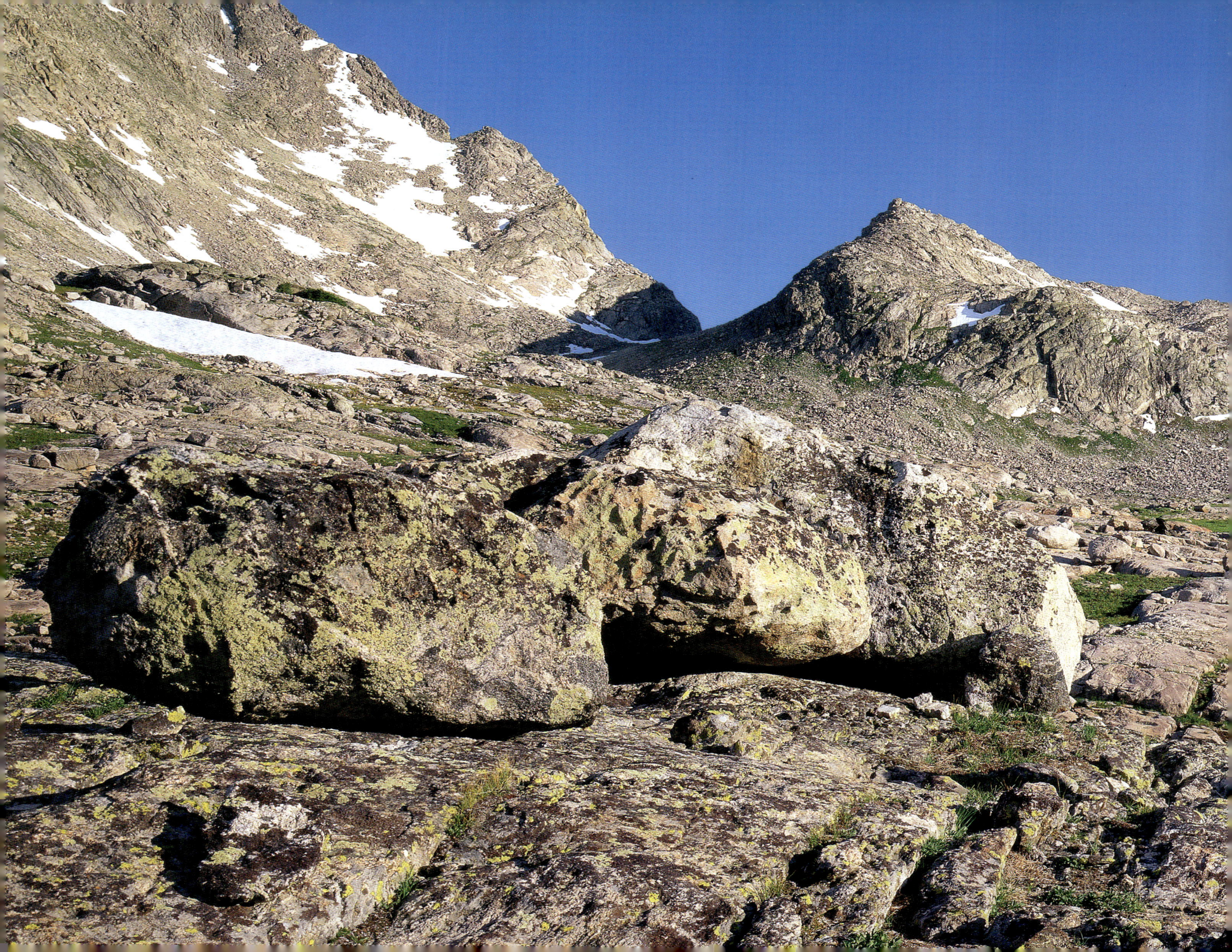

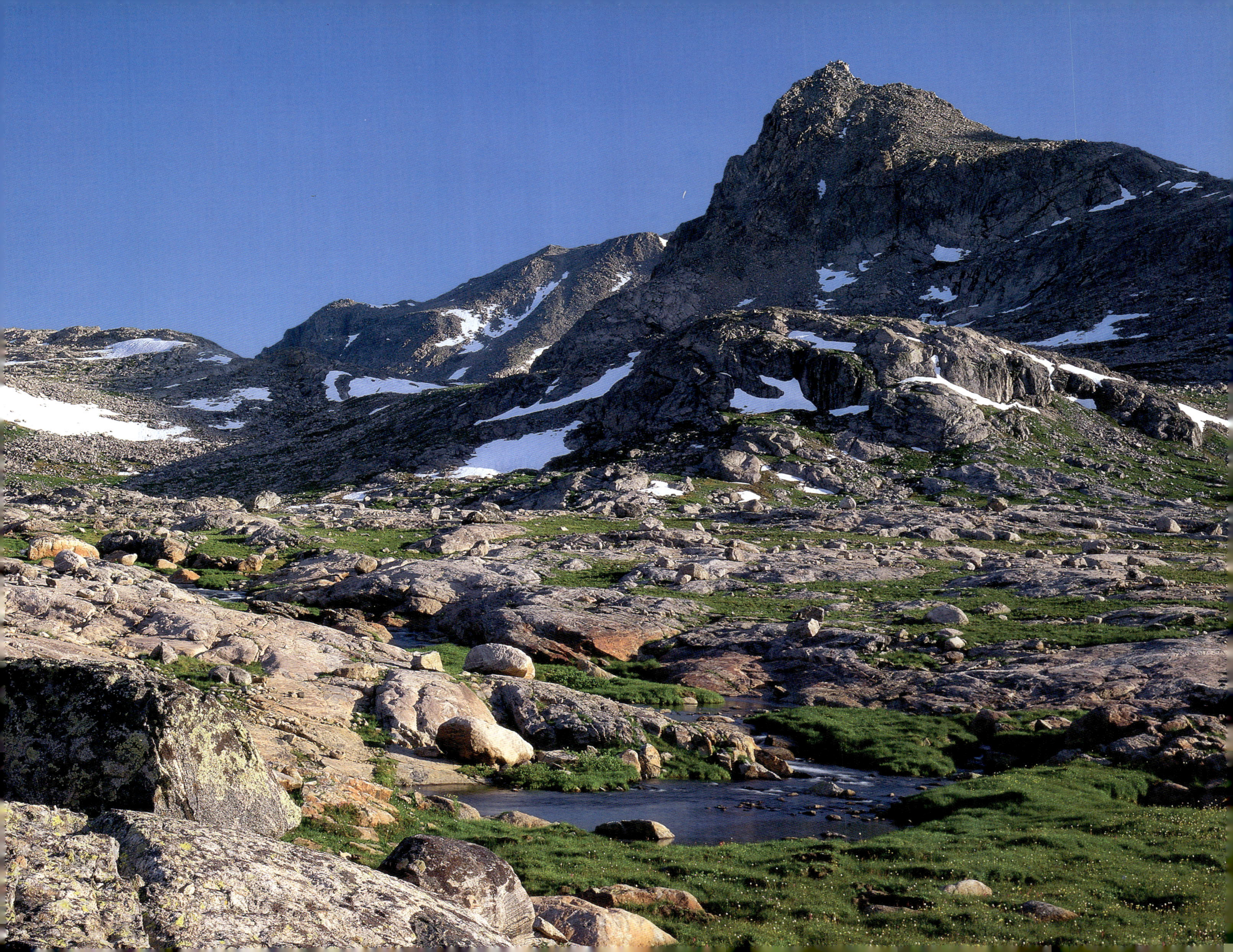

Moss and queen's crown sedum decorate Big Water Slide along Fremont Creek. Bridger Wilderness, Wind River Range, Bridger-Teton National Forest.

Previous page: A glacier-scoured basin below Shannon Pass. Bridger Wilderness, Wind River Range, Bridger-Teton National Forest.

Now confident that we can navigate Lester Pass, we load up the llamas and hit the trail before noon. Meltwater pours down the CDT below the pass. We find a passable notch in the cornice, although the snowfield is still steep. We lead the llamas, one by one, through the soft snow, kicking a dozen or so steps into the steepest lower edge of the drift. The llamas have no problems. Rocket is forgiven for bumping me. They are experienced packers so, even though they break through to their knees in several places, they remain unperturbed, and we soon gain the pass. We are the first party with pack stock to cross Lester Pass this year.

> *"We will traverse more than 40 miles of some of the most spectacular terrain in the Rocky Mountains, passing below the highest peaks in Wyoming and through the long, U-shaped valley of the upper Green River."*

I began using llamas for backcountry trips in the early 1990s when 90-pound backpacks full of too much large-format camera gear and too little good food became unbearable. I chose llamas because I know virtually nothing about horses. I find llamas ideally suited to my needs when photographing wild places. I would rather walk when I am making photos—I "see" better when I travel on my own feet—so I do not mind

Fog lingers along the Green River at sunrise. Bridger Wilderness, Wind River Range, Bridger-Teton National Forest.

Lupine and Indian paintbrush fill a meadow near the Continental Divide. Wind River Range, Shoshone National Forest.

that llamas are not ridable. They are very intelligent, easily managed beasts. Their size is less intimidating than that of a horse (mine range from about 300 to 345 pounds), and it makes them simple to transport. They can carry a surprising load. The three we have brought on this trip are loaded more heavily than I would like. Each left the trailhead with nearly 110 pounds. (I would have brought four llamas, but my small trailer only has room for three.) Relatives of the camel, they do well on little water and poor forage, enabling us to camp in places where horse packers can't. The soft pads on their two-toed feet make them surefooted and very easy on the trail. Best of all, they have a quality that is difficult to explain to anyone who has not spent time around llamas—a sort of Zen-like outlook on life that I find pleasing.

Fremont Peak

From Island Lake, on the west side of the Wind River Mountains, the 13,745-foot Fremont Peak fills the skyline. A massive, whale-backed peak on the Continental Divide, it dominates the view for many miles along the CDT and looms over the popular Titcomb Basin. It certainly looks like the highest peak in the range, but it is not. Five miles along the divide to the north, Gannett Peak is 59 feet higher, but it has a less commanding presence, hidden as it is behind the spires of migmitite and granite that crown the peaks at the head of Titcomb Basin.

Fremont Peak is named for John C. Frémont. In 1842, he and other members of his expedition reached its summit by scrambling up the southwest buttress. He believed it to be not only the highest peak in the range, but declared it to be the loftiest mountain in the Rockies. Never one to shy away from embellishing his feats of daring and prowess, he wrote in his report of how he "sprang upon the summit," an unlikely event given other descriptions of the party's long and difficult approach, near-debilitating altitude sickness, and a desperate traverse on hands and knees. It is doubtful that anyone does much leaping onto Fremont Peak or any of the high summits of the Wind River Range.

Fremont Peak rises above Island Lake. Bridger Wilderness, Wind River Range, Bridger-Teton National Forest.

An oil drill rig towers over grizzly bear habitat below Sheridan Pass. Shoshone National Forest.

A light rain begins to fall while we rest and grab a few handfuls of trail mix. The view to the north from Lester Pass is exceptional. Below is the cliff-bound defile of Titcomb Basin, its upper end surmounted by the 13,000-foot pinnacles, turrets, and pyramids of the Continental Divide. There is much vertical rock. Gannett Peak appears from this angle as a dome partly covered by ice, hinting at the large glaciers on the east side of the Divide. A member of John C. Frémont's 1842 exploration party described the landscape: "Around us the whole scene had one main striking feature, which was that of a terrible convulsion…"

Our standing as the only stock party over Lester Pass lasts for only 15 minutes. Just as we begin to descend, a string of horses appears carrying two outfitters and several wet, cold-looking clients, headed south over the pass for Pole Creek.

We camp at Island Lake, a mistake. It is on the Elkhart to Titcomb hiker highway and the area is badly overused: too many fire rings, too much trampled tundra, too many bright tents too close to the water. The next day we stop to examine Big Water Slide, a place where Fremont Creek pools, then roars down a smooth natural spillway of granite. The sound and motion mesmerize us.

Later we eat lunch at Upper Jean Lake, hunkered behind a rock outcrop in a snowstorm. Mary checks to see if the horse skeleton we discovered on our last trip is still near the edge of the lake. Some parts are missing, and some bones gnawed on, but the remains are where we found them last summer.

A year ago the skeleton was still perfectly articulated, flesh and hide neatly removed, but with metal shoes still on hooves and mane and tail intact. The skies were brilliant blue when we stopped for lunch in the lakeside meadow that day, and we staked out the llamas so they could graze. I was snapping some photos of the skeleton's big, toothy grin when I turned to find a fellow wearing thongs and neon purple shorts flip-flopping toward me, having appeared out of nowhere. He must have had a camp out of sight on one of the ledges above the lake. We didn't speak, just nodded, and then turned our attention to the bones at our feet. He assiduously studied the horse for a long moment, turned his gaze to the grazing llamas, then back to the skeleton. His brow furrowed and he spoke in a low, earnest voice: "They just don't seem to hold up as well as llamas, do they?" He then turned and flip-flopped back the way he came.

I repeat the quip to Shanna and Doug as we stand around the bones in the swirling flakes, and we laugh until our sides hurt. I am pleased with how well my llamas have held up and am glad they still look sturdy enough to carry food, film, cameras, and clothes all the way to Green River Lakes.

■ ■ ■

Cumulus clouds build above a tarn on the Continental Divide near Union Pass. Shoshone National Forest.

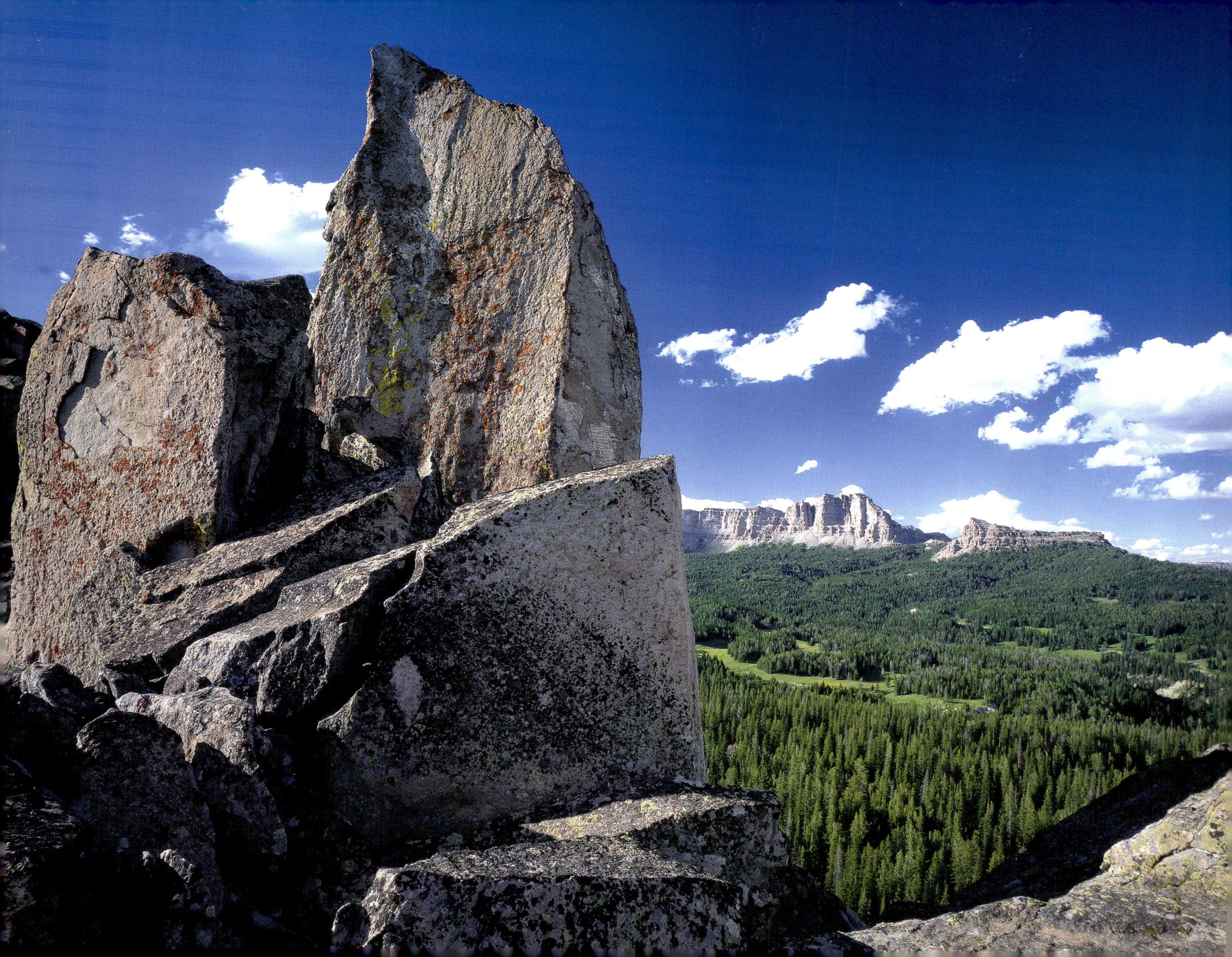

Greater Yellowstone

Teton Wilderness—September 1997

The lynching this evening went off without a hitch. My sister, Shanna, and I are pleased that two orange panniers are dangling from a noose of old climbing rope. An NBA star may be able to reach them with a running start, but we are hoping there are no grizzlies around that can reach 12 feet.

We are in the Greater Yellowstone Ecosystem—bear country—and wise travelers here practice a daily ritual: "The Hanging of the Food." (Actually, we entered bear country back in the Wind River Mountains. We hung the food there as well.) The necessary hoisting of the edibles reduces the chance of a bear encounter in camp. Bears are no dummies. If they discover that humans haul tasty bits into the woods, and that we silly bipeds are easy to chase or swat around, they can get aggressive about coming into camp. When that happens only bad outcomes are possible—torn-up gear and no food for the rest of your trip, scattered or mauled pack animals, injured or dead people, and, ultimately, the death of a bear that has become dangerous. The goal of putting the oatmeal and noodles up a tree is to avoid rewarding a curious bear's visit to camp.

The Hanging of the Food—a necessary tradition in bear country. Yellowstone National Park.

The Hanging of the Food sounds easy enough. Forest and Park Service brochures show how it is done. A diagram shows a handy branch at just the right height. It is long enough to keep things four feet from the trunk and sturdy enough to support the load. The branch in the illustration is horizontal and has no other branches around to interfere when you toss the rope over. Simply throw, hoist, and tie off to the easily accessible trunk of a nearby tree. And, of course, this hanging tree is exactly the required 100 yards from a wonderfully flat and grassy campsite.

The problem is, this ideal doesn't exist in the land of lodgepole and whitebark pines. The folks at Yellowstone recognize this and construct "bear poles" at their designated campsites. These are lodgepoles

Pinnacle Buttes and a forest viewed from the summit of Pilot Knob on the Continental Divide. Bridger-Teton National Forest.

Breccia Cliffs and Sublette Peak reflect in Brooks Lake. Shoshone National Forest.

lashed between two trees a dozen or so feet in the air. This makes the rope toss easier but still leaves room for plenty of comedy. Others may consistently accomplish The Hanging of the Food with no trouble, but I always look around to make sure nobody is lurking about with a video camera before I begin the slapstick.

> *"We're in the Greater Yellowstone Ecosystem—bear country—and wise travelers here practice a daily ritual: 'The Hanging of the Food.'"*

Here's how The Hanging of the Food goes in the real world (at least for me):

1. We find a camp with a level tent site and sufficient grazing for the llamas.

2. We unload our gear, then search for that perfect tree from the diagram.

3. After 30 minutes of stomping around meadow edges and through the woods, we settle for a tree a good deal farther from camp than 100 yards. It has a skinny branch that *might* support the weight. Other branches closely surround that branch, necessitating a precision rope toss.

4. I look around for a stone to tie my rope to. It must be small enough that I am able to lob it and the trailing strand to twice my height, but large enough so its weight can overcome

the friction of the line on the branch and so pull the rope's end down far enough for me to reach it on the other side. It takes a rock about the size of a grapefruit (Texas Ruby Red Jumbo). I look for one with "rope grooves," indentations that make the knot I tie around the rock more secure.

5. Now, the fun part. I take my nine-pound stone and try to heave it over only the chosen branch. If the rope goes over surrounding branches as well, this creates too much friction and it gets hung up. To perform a successful thread-the-needle toss nearly always requires many tries, and I am unable to maintain dignity because I run like hell after every throw. The reason for the rapid retreat is that sometimes the rock comes untied. I am still nursing (in September) what seems to be a broken rib acquired last July in the Wind River Range when the rock/rope combination went over a limb, started swinging back, and was suddenly a combination no more. The hefty projectile hit me below the collarbone before I could even flinch. Breathing at 10,000 feet still hurts.

6. More fun. Once the rope is over the branch, you have to hoist what can be a substantial load. Ours weighed nearly 90 pounds at the start of this trip. The combination of the weight and the friction of the rope may make it impossible to lift the food at all. You may watch a too-skinny branch bend, and what was supposed to hang at 10 feet dips to seven (and you hope that only short bears live nearby). Once up, a package that

Willows and a gently moving creek mark the landscape near Upper Brooks Lakes in the Absaroka Range. Shoshone National Forest.

Sunlight illuminates Brooks Lake Creek and Brooks Lake below the Breccia Cliffs. Absaroka Range, Shoshone National Forest.

A lodgepole pine seedling sprouts up amidst the aftermath of the 1988 fires. Yellowstone National Park.

heavy can make the lowering of the food an adventure for smaller campers, as my 120-pound little sister found when the counterweight jerked her off her feet.

All this may explain why we remember each day of our trip by how The Hanging of the Food went.

Day One. We hiked the nine miles to Heart Lake, stopping to eat lunch along the steaming thermal waters of Witch Creek. At the lake, our designated shoreline campsite had a bear pole and a nearby tent site. In a rush to get the food hung before an approaching thunderstorm arrived, I made a successful rock toss, but as I went to tie off the load, I tripped on a root and did a sort of Tarzan thing around the tree trunk. Shanna found this very amusing.

At dusk another electrical storm rolled over the summit of Mount Sheridan and across the lake. The show was spectacular, but things got a bit too interesting when bolts started hitting the slope above us.

An autumn rain drenches a meadow and conifers above the North Fork Buffalo Fork River drainage. A veiled Joy Peak towers in the distance. Teton Wilderness, Bridger-Teton National Forest.

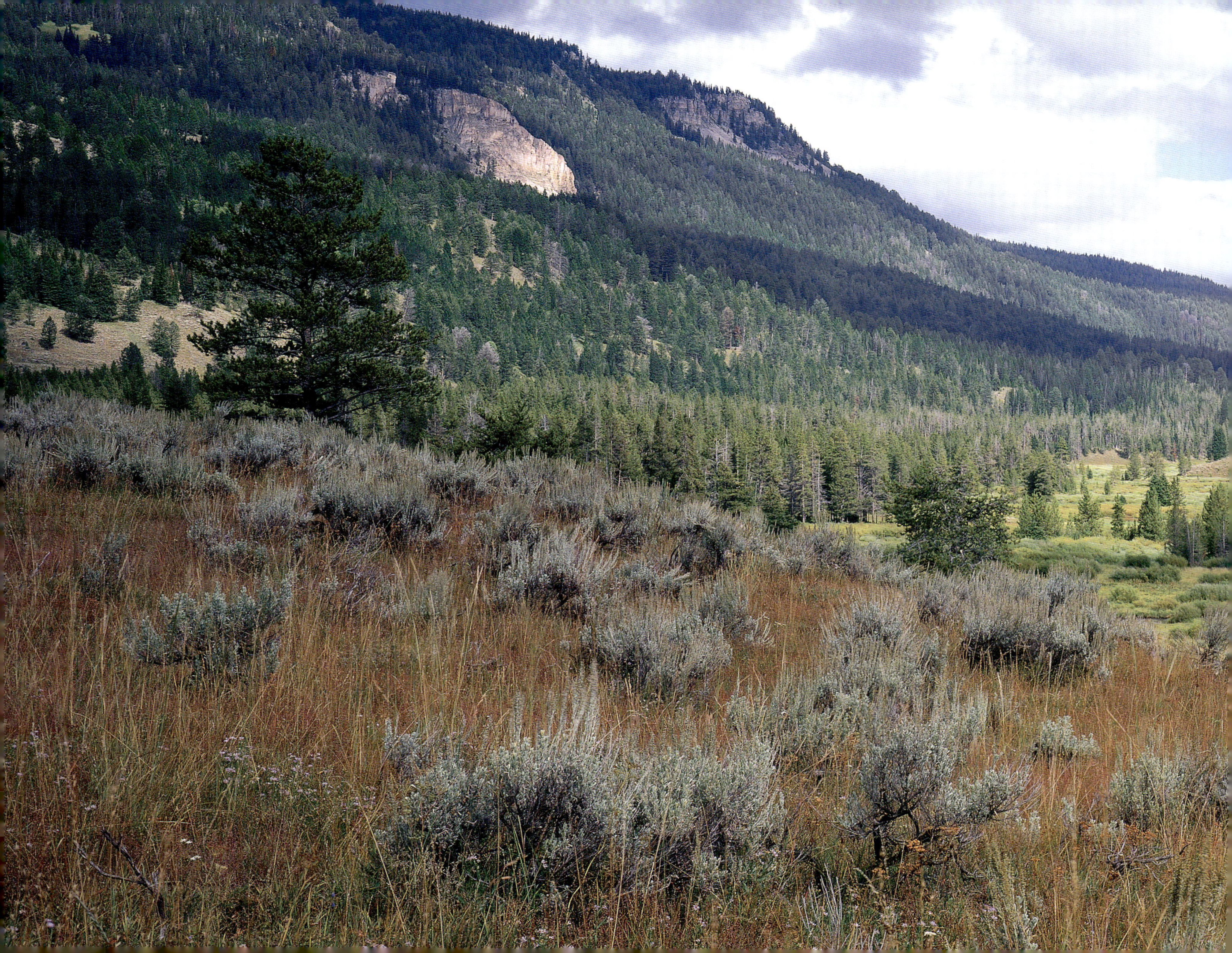

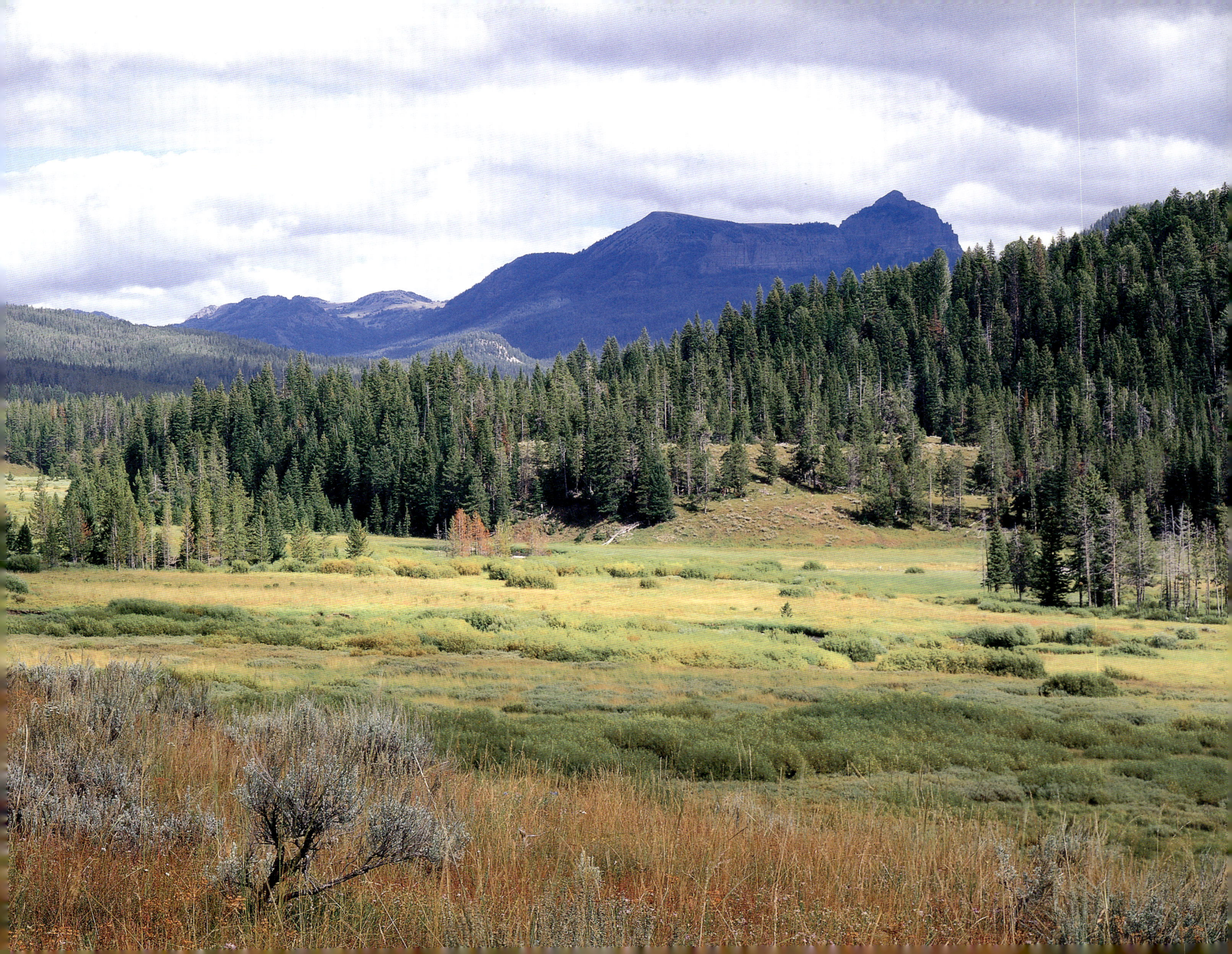

Mount Sheridan creates a backdrop for burned pine snags above Heart Lake. Yellowstone National Park.

Previous page: The distant Smokehouse Mountain reigns over the Soda Fork Meadows. Teton Wilderness, Bridger-Teton National Forest.

Columbia Spring near Heart Lake. Yellowstone National Park.

Day Two. We spent the morning backtracking along the shore of Heart Lake to have a look at Columbia Hot Spring and Rustic Geyser, which obligingly erupted for us. Back to camp at noon, we arrived at the tent just in time to take cover from a hailstorm. At the peak of the storm's intensity, lightning struck the surface of Heart Lake not 80 yards from us.

Having to hurry to reach our next official camp before dark, we descended the canyon of the Heart River to its junction with the Snake, passing too quickly through autumnal violet and yellow ground cover glowing below the burnished silver, bronze, and black trunks of trees burned in the 1988 fire.

We could not find the designated campsite. At sunset, another big cumulonimbus cloud boiled out of the southwest, lit a garish red, and both the sound of thunder and the

Yellowstone Lake at dusk. Yellowstone National Park.

A hiker crosses the Snake River in Fox Park. Teton Wilderness, Bridger-Teton National Forest.

Bison cross the Firehole River in Yellowstone National Park.

bugling of an elk echoed off the canyon walls. Trees started creaking and moaning ominously in a rising gale. In a bumpy clearing along the Snake, we got the llamas unloaded and the tent up just as lightning struck a pine on the canyon rim and more hail began to fall. My wide-eyed sister earnestly stated that she didn't know if she could stand it if her "Yellowstone Walkabout" continued at this intensity.

We did The Hanging in the dark. There was no bear pole, and the rope went over three branches. The friction was substantial and I had to loop the rope under my butt and lean with all my weight to move the bags at all. ("You need a bo's'n chair," advised my sister the sailor.) When I slipped and sat down in the mud, my sister again found it rather amusing.

Day Three. A much calmer day, thank you. We had a warm, sunny walk through the burn along the south-facing wall of the Snake River Canyon and found our assigned campsite to be level and grassy with bear pole in view. After we successfully suspended our panniers, I decided we needed a picture of The Hanging of the Food and asked Shanna to let the packs down and hoist them back up so I could get a shot. When she untied the rope, the weight lifted her off her feet. It was my turn to be amused.

Day Four. Before dawn we could hear five bull elk bugling in the clearings around us. At sunrise they ceased and a hike around camp after breakfast revealed none.

We crossed from the National Park into the Teton Wilderness while traversing the vast, grassy meadow of Fox Park. No more assigned camps (and no more bear poles). Along Mink Creek we found a good place to camp and a pretty good food-hanging branch, if a bit high. I had to make the stone toss through a small opening between branches. My first toss was too low and the second bounced off a branch and nearly beaned us. Neither of us found it amusing.

Bull elk and harem roam Yellowstone National Park.

A coyote comes into view on a Yellowstone National Park road turnout.

Day Five. We stopped for the day at the tree line on the ridge north of Two Ocean Pass. We were right on the Continental Divide and spectacular views made it a great camp—but what about The Hanging? At that elevation the only trees were a bunch of short, scraggly, wind-bent pines. And we had seen bear scat in the meadow a mile back. After some searching I found a distant tree that leaned out over a slope. It took a lot of rock throwing to get the rope placed right. Shanna was off watching elk bugle so she couldn't tell how amusing it was.

Day Six. We had lunch along North Two Ocean Creek at a very curious spot. As we watched, the creek split at the base of a conifer, with about one-third of the flow going west toward the Snake River and the Pacific Ocean, and the rest headed east toward the Yellowstone River and the Atlantic. One hundred and seventy years ago, no one believed mountain man Jim Bridger's story of fish swimming over mountains. His tale wasn't so tall. Recent DNA evidence indicates that the cutthroat trout in Yellowstone Lake are more closely related to the trout in the Snake River than in the Yellowstone River. Apparently fish *did* swim over the Continental Divide.

The afternoon brought evidence that significant rain was about to arrive. As the clouds lowered, we looked for a place to camp above the North Fork Buffalo Fork River. Good sites were scarce and good hanging trees even more so. We hoisted the food in a downpour as best we could, getting the panniers up, but not as high as I would have liked. With uncanny timing, a Forest Service wilderness ranger loped by in the rain not an hour later, and saw the panniers from the trail. He rode his horse into camp and we had a discussion about "10 feet high and four feet out from the trunk." Not wanting to argue with someone who was definitely *unamused*, I didn't suggest we march over and check things with a tape measure. I think we had 9 feet 8 inches. (He was right, and I had to admit it is better to have an irate, wet ranger in camp than a griz.)

A hiker offers directions at Parting of the Waters, where Two Ocean Creek splits on the Continental Divide.

That brings us to tonight's lynching. We moved the food to a new tree when the rain finally let up a bit, and had the best hanging of the trip. The rock was nicely notched and the knot secure. The rope went over the branch on the first throw, precisely where I wanted it. The panniers were light enough to hoist fairly easily.

We are hiking out to the trailhead at Turpin Meadows tomorrow. It seems that, on the last day of our walk, The Hanging of the Food may finally be without incident. Maybe. It is raining harder and the panniers and rope are growing heavier as they get wetter. The dead branch they are hanging from lets out a loud creak and pop.

Waves lap the shore of Shoshone Lake in Yellowstone National Park.

Old Faithful—June 1998

We came here to have a "Yellowstone Experience." This is our code phrase for the kind of fun you can have when you share nature with thousands of windshield tourists. The Continental Divide Trail (CDT) travels fearlessly through the heart of the small city surrounding Old Faithful geyser and so will we. Three million people visit Yellowstone every year; more than 600,000 will visit this month. It is a good bet that most of them stop at Old Faithful sometime during their stay.

For a long-distance hiker on the CDT, the transition from wilderness to "Park Service urban" must be nearly incomprehensible. After weeks or months of backcountry solitude, one suddenly emerges into something akin to Disney World on a busy day. If covering miles on the CDT is your only goal, you could sneak by in the dark, or slink through the woods, trying not to be noticed. But that's not what I advise. The Upper Geyser Basin is one of the wonders of the natural world. Boldly stride across a parking lot bigger than Wal-Mart's and watch Old Faithful erupt. Spend a few hours geyser-gazing along the boardwalks before you slip onto the Madison Plateau and vanish into the forest.

Mary and I, with Doug and Shanna, are going to spend a week in Yellowstone being dutiful automobile tourists. We will spend most of the time photographing thermal features along the CDT in the Upper Geyser Basin. Doug has never been to the park and wants to see as much hot water and steam as possible. We expect him to be appropriately wowed.

Kepler Cascades surge along the Firehole River in Yellowstone National Park.

I have a Yellowstone Experience even before we get to Old Faithful. We have camped at Lewis Lake near where the CDT crosses the South Entrance Road on the way to Shoshone Lake. I am walking along the campground road at dawn on a very cold, foggy morning, intent on photographing the dead trees along the CDT. At the park road I have to leap out of the way as a truck carrying a very large camper careens into the campground. The truck screeches to a stop and the passenger side door bursts open. A little man, barely five feet tall, dressed in full fly-fishing regalia sprints toward me, waving his hands and shouting, "Hey! Hey! You from Newport, Rhode Island?"

Speechless, I can only shake my head. "Oh. I thought you was," he says sadly, and jogs back to the truck. I have just been accosted by a gnome. It's hard to imagine that happening back in the Great Divide Basin.

The pools and geysers in the Upper Geyser Basin are as wondrous as ever. Unbelievable. Astounding. Fascinating. Miraculous. No words can really do them justice. Standing in the heat and steam blowing off a sapphire pool as the landscape dims and blurs is a mystical experience, a journey back in time to a younger, wilder Earth.

A lone fisherman tries his skill in the Firehole River. Yellowstone National Park.

We watch several eruptions of Old Faithful. I have observed this famous geyser hundreds of times and never grow tired of it. What can you say about something that not only blows water and steam hundreds of feet into the air, but does so according to a conveniently posted schedule?

Not everyone is impressed. After one eruption, two young men complain, "We waited 20 minutes for *that*?"

Following another, a woman turns to a ranger and asks in a dissatisfied voice, "Was that *it*?"

I worry about why so many find Old Faithful disappointing. Why does something I always find amazing not meet these people's expectations? And how much am I to blame? To be successful, a landscape photographer must capture the world at its most spectacular. Scenes must look "better than real." I have photographed Old Faithful many times and still don't have an image I am particularly pleased with. But when I do get one, it is likely to be published widely. People are bombarded with thousands of these perfect images in books, on cards, on TV and video cassette. Each image may represent weeks or months of a photographer's patient waiting until all elements come together. Yet many visitors to

Wildflowers pepper the Continental Divide above Two Ocean Pass. Teton Wilderness, Bridger-Teton National Forest.

A morning fog enshrouds the remains of these trees, killed by thermal water, in the Upper Geyser Basin. Yellowstone National Park.

Yellowstone will see Old Faithful erupt only once before rushing off to the Grand Tetons, Zion Canyon, Yosemite. They have been set up for disappointment.

As we walk down the boardwalk, my gloomy reverie depresses me. Then I see something that brightens my mood considerably. It is a little boy, about four years old, who is so excited to be here he can hardly stand it. He has no preconceived notions about how Yellowstone should look. He stops every dozen feet to bend over, hands on knees, and examine something: a pine cone, a steaming fumarole, a bison track. He directs a rapid stream of "Why?" and "What?" questions to his parents. It is a shame that the adults here (myself included) have not retained more of this child's wonder.

We have another Yellowstone Experience farther down the boardwalk. Shanna has been reading to us from our book about geysers and a couple has overheard. They approach, apparently regarding us as Yellowstone experts. The woman wants to know if they can see the Grand Teton here or whether they have to actually go there. We look confused so she tries to clarify: "We paid an entrance fee for Yellowstone *and* Grand Teton National Park."

Our third Yellowstone Experience is a typical one. An "animal jam." Any large wildlife along a park road creates an instant traffic tie-up as folks stop to look and take snapshots. If you spend enough time driving in Yellowstone you can get a good idea about what kind of animal it is by how the cars are parked. If they have pulled all the way onto the shoulder, it is

Mystic Falls cascade along the Little Firehole River in Yellowstone National Park.

GREATER YELLOWSTONE 81

Old Faithful Geyser erupts right on schedule. Upper Geyser Basin, Yellowstone National Park.

Geysers

Yellowstone National Park contains more than half the world's geysers. The park's Upper Geyser Basin alone contains more than 200 geysers—better than 20 percent of all the geysers on the planet consolidated in an area of 1.5 square miles. It was probably the Upper Geyser Basin, above all else, that led to Yellowstone's designation as the first National Park in 1872.

A wonderful variety of geysers is found in Yellowstone: small, nearly perpetual spouters; giants hundreds of feet high that erupt rarely and erratically; fountains bursting from pools; steady columns rising from sintered cones. Whatever type of geyser, you will likely find the best example here.

Geysers need three things to exist: a supply of water, potent geothermal heat, and a special plumbing system. Ample precipitation falls on the high Yellowstone Plateau, providing groundwater. The Earth's internal heat is particularly close to the surface at Yellowstone. But the key is silica-rich rhyolite the volcanic rock that covers much of Yellowstone. Virtually all geysers are found within large, geologically recent deposits of rhyolite and such volcanic fields exist in few places. Rhyolite produces plumbing of the correct shape, lined with minerals strong enough to withstand tremendous pressure, and with enough permeable volume to hold the huge amounts of water that geysers eject during an eruption.

Geysers are very dynamic. The slightest changes in the geologic environment may radically alter any of them. Although nobody knows why, observers in Yellowstone have counted more active geysers in recent years than ever before in recorded history.

Steam rises from geothermal features along the Firehole River in Yellowstone National Park.

"Standing in the heat and steam blowing off a sapphire pool as the landscape dims and blurs is a mystical experience, a journey back in time to a younger, wilder Earth."

A frosted spider web glistens in the morning fog. Upper Geyser Basin, Yellowstone National Park.

probably something common like bison or elk. If vehicles have been parked more hastily, with rear ends protruding into the traffic lane, it may be a bull elk or moose with really big antlers, or perhaps a hunting coyote. Cars stopped right in the traffic lane and people running along the road mean a bear or a wolf.

Our animal jam includes several crookedly parked RVs and, sure enough, there are two bull elk with large, velvet-covered racks sauntering through the pines. We park the truck (all the way off the road) and join the throng to watch and snap a few shots with a telephoto lens.

Then we're off to our destination. We are having fun being tourists. Our aim is to wear big grins as we take a photo of ourselves standing in front of a sign that reads: CONTINENTAL DIVIDE, ELEVATION 8,391.

The cone of Castle Geyser spews steam above Tortoiseshell Spring. Upper Geyser Basin, Yellowstone National Park.

Steam rises from Sapphire Pool in Biscuit Basin. Yellowstone National Park.

Appendices

■ Bibliography and Suggested Reading ■

Adkison, Ron. *Hiking Wyoming's Wind River Range*. Helena, Montana: Falcon Press Publishing Co., Inc., 1996.

Alter, J. Cecil. *Jim Bridger*. Norman, Oklahoma: University of Oklahoma Press, 1979.

Berger, Karen and Daniel R. Smith. *Where the Waters Divide: A 3,000 Mile Trek Along America's Continental Divide*. Woodstock, Vermont: The Countryman Press, 1997.

Bryan, T. Scott. *Geysers of Yellowstone*. Niwot, Colorado: University Press of Colorado, 1995.

Ferguson, Gary. *Walking Down the Wild: A Journey Through the Yellowstone Rockies*. New York: Simon & Schuster, 1993.

Lageson, David R. and Darwin R. Spearing. *Roadside Geology of Wyoming*. Missoula, Montana: Mountain Press Publishing Company, 1988.

Lamar, Howard Roberts, ed. *The New Encyclopedia of the American West*. New Haven, Connecticut: Yale University Press, 1998.

Moulton, Candy. *Roadside History of Wyoming*. Missoula, Montana: Mountain Press Publishing Company, 1995.

Rawlins, C. L. *Sky's Witness: A Year in the Wind River Range*. New York: Henry Holt and Company, 1992.

Robbins, Michael and Paul Chesley. *High Country Trail: Along the Continental Divide*. Washington, D.C.: National Geographic Society, 1981.

■ Conservation and Trail Advocacy Groups ■

Continental Divide Trail Alliance (CDTA)
P.O. Box 628
Pine, CO 80470
(888) 909-CDTA
E-mail: CDNST@aol.com
Web: www.cdtrail.org

Continental Divide Trail Society (CDTS)
3704 N. Charles St., #601
Baltimore, MD 21218
(410) 235-9610
E-mail: cdtsociety@aol.com
Web: www.gorp.com/cdts

Greater Yellowstone Coalition
P.O. Box 1874
Bozeman, MT 59771
(406) 586-1593
E-mail: gyc@greateryellowstone.org
Web: www.greateryellowstone.org

International Llama Association
7853 E. Arapahoe Ct., #2100
Englewood, CO 80112
(800) WHY-LAMA (949-5262)
Fax: (303) 694-4869
E-mail: ila@internationallama.org
Web: www.internationallama.org

The Nature Conservancy, Wyoming Chapter
258 Main St., Ste. 200
Lander, WY 82520
(307) 332-2971
Web: www.tnc.org

**Sierra Club
North Plains Region**
23 N. Scott St., #27
Sheridan, WY 82801-6336
(307) 672-0425

Wind River Backcountry Horseman
c/o Dick Inberg
P.O. Box 1751
Riverton, WY 82501
(307) 856-1657

Wyoming Outdoor Council
262 Lincoln St.
Lander, WY 82520
(307) 332-7031
Web: www.wocnet.org

History of the Continental Divide National Scenic Trail

The Continental Divide National Scenic Trail (CDNST) began in 1966 as the dream of Benton MacKaye, an 87-year-old man who had already devoted much of his life to seeing the Appalachian Trail come to fruition. MacKaye's idea was to create a trail that would connect a series of wilderness areas along the Divide from Montana's border with Canada to New Mexico's border with Mexico.

MacKaye (rhymes with "deny") proposed his idea to Congress, which soon authorized a study of the trail under the National Trails Act of 1968. At around the same time, a Baltimore attorney by the name of Jim Wolf was hiking the 2,000-mile-long Appalachian Trail, which he completed in 1971. Inspired to seek out a new hiking challenge further afield, Wolf walked the Divide Trail from the Canadian border to Rogers Pass, Montana, in 1973. He soon published a guidebook covering that section of the trail and devoted much of his time to advocating its official designation. After a 1976 study by the Bureau of Outdoor Recreation found the scenic quality of the trail to surpass anything available anywhere else in the country, the Congressional Oversight Committee of the National Trail System held hearings on the trail in 1978, at which Wolf testified. The CDNST received official recognition from Congress later that year under the National Parks and Recreation Act.

In that same year, Wolf founded the Continental Divide Trail Society (CDTS) to garner publicity for the trail and involve the public in work surrounding its construction, particularly its route selection. Wolf continued to hike portions of the trail each summer, and by the mid-'80s he had completed all of its 3,100 miles.

The United States Forest Service is responsible for managing most of the land through which the trail passes. In the 1980s, its work on the trail progressed at different rates in different areas, but it suffered in general from a lack of public involvement. In 1994, two trail advocates began working under the auspices of a group called the Fausel Foundation to raise funds and build support for the trail. By 1995, their efforts evolved into the Continental Divide Trail Alliance (CDTA), a nonprofit organization devoted to fund-raising, publicity, education about the trail, and grassroots volunteer coordination. The CDTA founders were Bruce Ward, formerly the president of the American Hiking Society, and his wife, Paula, a landscape architect.

In its first year, the CDTA grew to include 425 individuals or families, 20 corporate sponsors, and a budget of $400,000. Estimates suggest the Alliance coordinated volunteer work worth $70,000 in that first year. However, trail advocates are quick to point out that there is much work yet to be done. Completion and maintenance of the trail will require funding and volunteer coordination throughout the 21st century.

GENEROUSLY CONTRIBUTED BY TOM LORANG JONES
Revised from *Colorado's Continental Divide Trail: The Official Guide*

The Continental Divide Trail Alliance
Protecting a Vital National Resource

How can you help?
By becoming a member of the Continental Divide Trail Alliance (CDTA). Your willingness to join thousands of concerned citizens across the country will make the difference. Together, we can provide the financial resources needed to complete the trail.

CDTA is a nonprofit membership organization formed to help protect, build, maintain, and manage the CDT. CDTA serves a broad-based constituency and includes people who enjoy recreating on public lands, as well as those concerned about overdevelopment.

As a CDTA member, you will:

- Protect a vital and precious natural resource
- Ensure trail maintenance and completion
- Improve trail access
- Support informational and educational programs
- Champion volunteer projects
- Advocate for policy issues that support the CDT

What does it take to help us? Just one cent a mile.
We realize there are a lot of demands on your time and budget. That's why we're only asking you to give a little—just one cent a mile to support the Trail. For a modest membership fee of $31, you will help us go so very far, and finish what was courageously started so long ago.

For more information or to send your contribution, write to:

Continental Divide Trail Alliance
P.O. Box 628
Pine, CO 80470
(888) 909-CDTA
www.cdtrail.org

Please make checks payable to CDTA.

Following page: Cumulus clouds hover above an autumn meadow and forest along the Howard Eaton Trail. Yellowstone National Park.